AL BOWLLY

Also by Sid Colin
And The Bands Played On

AL BOWLLY

Sid Colin and Tony Staveacre

WITH A FOREWORD BY
DENIS NORDEN

ELM TREE BOOKS
LONDON

First published in Great Britain 1979
by Elm Tree Books/Hamish Hamilton Ltd
Garden House, 57–59 Long Acre London WC2E 9JL
Copyright © 1979 by Sid Colin and Tony Staveacre
British Library Cataloguing in Publication Data
Colin, Sid
  Al Bowlly.
  1. Bowlly, Al 2. Singers – Biography
  I. Staveacre, Tony
  784'.092'4   ML420.B/
  ISBN 0 241 10057 7

Printed in Great Britain by
Ebenezer Baylis & Son Ltd,
The Trinity Press, Worcester, and London

CONTENTS

Acknowledgments — vii
Foreword by Denis Norden — ix
Jockey with a Banjo — 1
Stomping at the Savoy — 15
Brother, Can You Spare a Dime? — 27
The Magic Circle — 34
White Tie and Tails — 39
The Hostess with the Mostest — 49
Top of the Bill — 56
Champagne and Strawberries — 71
Sixty-five Stories Nearer the Stars — 81
Welcome Home — 94
A Charmed Life — 105
Discography by Brian Rust and Clifford Harvey — 111
Index — 161

ACKNOWLEDGMENTS

We are indebted to many people for sharing with us their memories of Al Bowlly. Among them we must especially thank Roy Fox, Joyce Stone, Monia Liter, Joe Crossman, Nat Gonella, Tiny Winters, Anona Winn, Norman Payne, Harry Hayes, Hilda and Leslie Harding, the late Don Barrigo and the late Ray Noble.

An especial thank you to Melody Maker for allowing us to use their files and quote from past publications; and to the following authors and their works for information about people and places which make an appearance in this book; *The Long Party* by Stella Margetson (Saxon House, 1974); *The Big Bands* (Collier Macmillan 1975) and *Glenn Miller and his Orchestra* (T. Y. Crowell, 1974) by George T. Simon; *The Dance Band Era* by Albert McCarthy (Chiltern Book Co., 1971).

Our thanks too to Brian Rust and Clifford M. Harvey for compiling the Al Bowlly discography, reproduced here by kind permission of Arlington House, New York, and to the following sources for the illustrations used: 1. Monia Liter; 2, 3, 4, 5, 8, 10, 11, 12, 13, 14, 16, Jazz Music Books; 6, 7, Mrs Joyce Stone; 15, Nat Gonella; 9, Tiny Winters.

FOREWORD
by Denis Norden

For a couple of weeks in 1968 I found myself involved in a project to make a film based on the life of Al Bowlly. During his ritual Saturday afternoon cruising of Portobello Market, one of a group of glitteringly successful American film-producers who lived in London at that time had picked up Bowlly's recording of 'Sweet As A Song'. Even though the singer's name was completely unfamiliar to him, something about the voice sent him in search of more Al Bowlly 78s. By the time I was summoned to his office he'd acquired an impressive stack of them.

'Want you to listen to something,' he said and put the Lew Stone version of 'I'll Never Be The Same' on the record-player. We listened. 'Isn't that a strange voice?' the producer said. 'A *strange* voice.'

I said, 'It's Al Bowlly.' For some reason, it came out sounding defensive.

The producer nodded. He pointed a finger at me, the way they do when they're about to reveal the secret of it all. 'He comes on the way Bogie came on.'

I didn't understand the comparison at the time, mainly because I thought it had something to do with toughness. 'I keep wondering if there's a movie there,' the producer said. 'Know anything about him?'

I didn't know much but I was able to put him in touch with people who did – including Sid Colin and a privately printed magazine called *Golden Years* which dwells so lovingly on the dance-bands of the 1930s and the 1940s that you can even read learned articles about the musical influences on Bram Martin.

The project never came to anything. 'They're not ready for it,' the producer said regretfully after all the research material was in. 'It's a story about a loser. There's no Third Act.'

Five years later I was conscripted to run an afternoon TV programme called *Looks Familiar*, an exercise in show-business archaeology designed to put popular entertainers of the thirties and forties back on display. Because I was inclined to the theory that nostalgia works best when it's ironical, I tended to exhibit a fairly light attitude towards these yellowing valentines; but it soon became apparent that there are certain artists of that period who retain an astonishingly fierce hold on the emotions of middle-aged viewers. Jack Buchanan and Sid Field are two such names, but it was only when anything to do with Bogart or Bowlly was shown on the programme that I was made aware of what might be called the *erogenous* zones of nostalgia: you only have to touch on them and arousal takes place. As one Wedgwood-haired lady said to me after a show in which we'd had Bowlly singing 'Melancholy Baby', 'Whenever I hear his voice, it just melts in my mouth!'

That was when I began acquiring more respect for the film-producer's instincts. A further five years on, and another of his judgments on Bowlly – 'It's a story about a loser' – was lent some weight. The BBC showed Dennis Potter's complex action replay of the 1930s, the series of TV plays called *Pennies From Heaven*. Although its title was a song we associate mainly with Bing Crosby, the insistent voice throughout was that of Al Bowlly. Even more relevant was the hero of the series. Stubbily broad-shouldered, oiled-back hair, his carnality shot through with dreams of white dinner-jackets and camel coats draped over the shoulders, he was tuned to the exact note of loser's jauntiness we hear throughout this biography.

It was the biography that confirmed the producer's final words on Bowlly. His life did lack the requisite Third Act. Up from singing in the streets to singing on the biggest network radio programme in America, down again to second spot after the interval at the Rex, High Wycombe – then, abruptly, The End.

It is a loser's story. The puzzle about it, though, the question that vaguely troubles those of us who were around when he was, is why the sound of his voice still 'works'. (Even on an American who'd never heard of him before.) Why, out of all the singers of his day, was Al Bowlly the one who got into a generation's bloodstream?

It's a question that requires really thoughtful evasion. The authors of this scrupulously detailed memoir were as correct in not even attempting to answer it as they were wrong in hoping I would. As I write this piece I've got Bowlly on the table behind me singing 'Faint Harmony' (one of his best, recorded in 1934 with the Lew Stone Band) but I still can't discern where the secret lies. There's no denying the tunefulness of the voice, with its unmistakable overlay of both the nasal and the reedy, yet there is a certain thinness to it and I can remember at least three other dance-band singers of that time who, judged purely in terms of vocal quality, must surely rate higher. But – and this is one of the places where the mystery of nostalgia lives – would any 'Faint Harmony' of theirs evoke such an immediate recall of hanging about outside the gates of Clissold Park, waiting for a girl called Fenella Silver?

Someone given to writing such things once wrote that 'Memory is a crazed woman who hoards coloured beads and throws away food.' If that's true, then any of you who lived through the Bowlly years will probably supply your own thread for stringing together all the coloured beads scattered about this affectionate book. On the other hand, it may only be you others – the ones for whom Al Bowlly is just a name on nostalgia programmes – who can provide the linking thread. It could be that the way nostalgia really works best is if you weren't there first time round.

DENIS NORDEN
July 1978

Jockey with a Banjo

He was essentially a very private person. Even at the height of his fame, he was disinclined to reveal too much about himself, leaving his chroniclers to piece the story together from a number of eccentric and often-contradictory sources. Of his early years on the other side of the world, there are few first-hand reports to balance against the myths and legends which have sprung up since his death, and which now obscure our view of the boyhood of Bowlly.

It is certain that he was born in Lourenço Marques, on the East Coast of Africa. The date of his birth, however, is variously given as 1890, 1898, 1901—even 1906. On his death certificate, the date of birth is recorded as 7 January 1898: but then it appears that in middle age he was inclined to knock a few years off (who wants to know a crooner when he's fifty?). The weight of evidence seems to point to 1890, which is the date given in a printed concert programme for the Elizalde Orchestra, at the Shepherds Bush Empire in 1929. According to Lew Stone, who had to fill in a work-permit form for Al in 1932, he was then secretly admitting to forty-two. His contemporaries from those days remember teasing him as 'the Daddy of the Band'; while they—Nat Gonella, Tiny Winters, Joe Crossman, Monia Liter—are now in their early seventies, Al Bowlly, if *he* were still alive, would be nearly ninety.

His father came from Rhodes and his mother was Lebanese. They met on a ship bound for Australia and were married in Adelaide. From there they moved on to South Africa, and Al—christened Albert Alick and the fourth of their ten children—was born shortly after the family had arrived in Lourenço Marques, in what was then Portuguese East Africa (now Mozambique). A year later they moved to Durban, and from there to Johannesburg, where they settled; Al's younger brother Misch still lives there today.

The children were sent to the Newtown school, which was attended by British, Dutch-Boer and coloured children, so Al's mixed parentage caused no particular problems. In later years it was to provoke some speculation about his origins, and was the cause of embarrassment to Al, who became enthusiastically pro-British and was disinclined to acknowledge his exotic roots. His lady admirers describe him as 'foreign-looking', with olive-coloured skin and masses of black hair. Roy Fox compares him to Rudolph Valentino: Al had 'that same Latin style and appearance'. In 1935, Ray Noble was amazed to discover a colony of Al's relatives living in Massachusetts where 'the girls were still wearing yashmaks!'.

As a child, Al was tough, independent, excitable; always spoiling for a fight, good at sport, but academically dull. Recalling his schooldays, he described himself as a 'real little ruffian'. When he was nine, his father, who was having some difficulty supporting ten children on a store-keeper's wage, sent young Al out to work after school as a lather-boy in his uncle's barbershop. At fourteen, he left school to work there full-time and learn the trade. He also learned how to play the ukelele and, according to one of the often repeated Al Bowlly legends, he became known as 'the singing barber' because of his impromptu performances for waiting customers. It's a nice story and might well be true.

There is little evidence to suggest what it was that aroused Al's interest in music, nor is it easy to form a clear picture of what *kind* of music a teenaged, mixed-race boy would have been exposed to in Johannesburg at the turn of the century, where so many different cultural influences were coming together. Vast numbers of slaves were being imported (especially from Malaya) to work alongside the native Kaffirs in the gold mines: together they created their own 'work-music', with the result that prejudices later developed against Afrikaans folk music. It was considered to be beneath the dignity of the white man. The British settlers, who had arrived in significant numbers since 1820, had brought their own musical traditions with them: church music, parlour songs, folk songs. Some of these were translated into Afrikaans and became part of the popular music repertoire. '*Sy was Arm maar Sy was Eirlik*'—'She was Poor but She was Honest'—was one such song which, curiously, appears in the Al Bowlly Discography as having been recorded by him in Afrikaans, under the name of Jannie Viljoen, in London in 1930. (Decca didn't like the recording, so it was never released.)

The Dutch-Boers had their own tradition of *boeremusiek*—music for dances, picnics and celebrations—and played on the concertina, fiddle and guitar. They had their own songs, too. The Boer War inspired a number of jingoistic songs like '*Mij Hemelland*' ('My Homeland') and '*Banditlied*' ('The Prisoner's Song'). When the war was over, the musical invasion continued. Stars of the English music hall toured South Africa with the songs they had made famous at home: Lottie Collins with her explosive 'Ta-Ra-Ra-Boom-De-Ay!' and Eugene Stratton with his delicate 'Lily of Laguna'. Musical comedy followed: elegant Edwardian confections, like Leslie Stuart's 'Floradora', were acclaimed by enthusiastic audiences in Cape Town and Johannesburg. From America, via London, came the minstrel shows—'the Ethiopian Serenaders', 'the Mohawks', 'McNish, Johnson and Slavin's Refined Minstrels'—presenting their 'ideal programme' of ballads, comic songs and repartee. Much later, there would be ragtime, jazz and dance music, but by then the invention of the gramophone had turned the trickle of imported music into a flood.

How much of all this had any significance for Al Bowlly, part-time would-be ukelele player? There's no doubt that he enjoyed the Victorian church music of his schooldays—he sang in the choir, and remained a devout Christian all his life. He would certainly have had more opportunity to hear the mine-boys with their guitars than the visiting stars from London. And in later years, far from home, he could still sing in Afrikaans of his 'Homestead (*Woorhuis*) in the Valley of Dreams (*Droomvallei*)'. It's quite probable that he played in a *boerorke* at picnics and parties, and it's easy to imagine him frequenting Eloff Street, which was Johannesburg's Tin Pan Alley, searching for the newly arrived American jazz records. By then, of course, he would have been in his twenties and running his own barbershop, but perhaps beginning to consider the possibility of becoming a professional musician. He had progressed from the ukelele, and could now play the banjo and, less expertly, the guitar (the banjo always remained his favourite instrument). He got a part-time job as a banjoist in a small orchestra which played dance music in a Jo'burg café. And it was there that, one night, opportunity presented itself Hollywood-style. The bandleader, hearing his banjo player quietly humming the choruses to himself, invited him to 'get up and sing', which Al duly did. A colleague from that band later recalled (in *Melody Maker*, July 1934) that 'the ladies loved him, and he soon became a local celebrity!'. But his singing style was not, apparently, universally appreciated. The secretary of a smart Jo'burg club complained to the leader after the band's first performance there: 'Is it necessary to have that man who plays the thingummyjig make those awful noises? It's ghastly! Listen, if your band wants to keep its job, tell that fellow to stick to his banjo and cut out the funny noises.'

He certainly had a distinctive singing style: on record, his voice is always immediately recognizable. He was a 'falsetto tenor', and had a remarkable range. But perhaps it was because he sang rather softly that, in those early pre-microphone days, he had some difficulty in selling himself as a singer. In the 1920s, Al Jolson was the king. In comparison with Jolson's forceful, shouting, vocal style, Al Bowlly's gentle murmurings were considered rather 'cissy'. The crooner, who sang 'like a mother crooning quietly to her baby', would have to wait for the invention of the electric amplifier before he could really come into his own.

Even so, Al Bowlly's first forays into the Jo'burg dance-band scene caused a few tremors in the opposition. Edgar Adeler was the top man in the business at the time: his 'Syncopators' were considered to be the best American-style band in town, and he also ran a number of subsidiary bands, providing music for official functions and big social occasions. When Adeler heard of Al Bowlly's growing popularity, he took the sensible precaution of offering him a job—even though his band already included a vocalist, Johnny Jacobs, and a very fine sixteen year old banjo player, Len Fillis. Al joined Adeler, reverting to his ukelele for the instrumental numbers, and singing some vocals. The band played at the Lounge Tea Rooms every afternoon and three evenings a week. The musicians were guaranteed a minimum of £10 per week, which they doubled with extra gigs at the weekend. Al Bowlly was now a professional musician.

In 1923, Adeler set his sights on London. The plan was to work his passage by playing en route—round the East Coast of Africa, through the Suez Canal and on to England. The musicians jumped at the idea. Adeler guaranteed to pay all expenses, after which they would split any profits five ways: Adeler (pianist), Johnny Jacobs (violin and vocals), Len Fillis (tenor banjo), Desmond Gregg (percussion doubling alto saxophone), and Al Bowlly (vocals and ukelele). The first stage of their route was planned—Mafeking, Francistown, Bulawayo, Broken Hill, Salisbury and Mombasa. The band made their farewells, and Al Bowlly sold his barbershop. He was thirty-three when he left home for the first time. He never went back.

In Mafeking the band split £50 for a one-night stand. As they progressed up the coast, the bush telegraph signalled their approach and white settlers, planters and farmers, who had never heard the new jazz music played 'live', came flocking. In Bulawayo, Len Fillis announced that he was leaving the band, so Adeler called in Bowlly and told him to get his banjo out and start practising again. When Fillis made his exit, Al stepped into his place.

In Mombasa, Adeler received a cable inviting him to tour India for twelve months. Although England was the band's ultimate goal, the offer seemed too good to refuse. In the spring of 1924, they set sail for Bombay, but without Johnny Jacobs, who went back to Johannesburg to take charge of Adeler's second band. His place was taken by a young violinist from London called Ernie Kapinsky (he later became Ernie Lewis). As the new violinist was not a singer, Al Bowlly was now vocalist-in-chief. His big number was 'Yes, We Have No Bananas!'.

The band syncopated their way across the Indian continent and through the Khyber Pass, untroubled by local disturbances or warring tribal chieftains. Then on to Burma, and the Malay States. In Sourabaya, tempers flared. During Adeler's piano solo, Al Bowlly threw a cushion at him, in full view of the audience.

Adeler was furious, and when the band came off stage, he hit Al. Al replied in kind and the two men laid into one another until the other musicians pulled them apart. Adeler, still seething, fired him on the spot.

This incident provides the first evidence of Al's excitable—even violent—nature. In later years he was notorious for carrying a dangerously short fuse; when he was roused, the veins would stand out on his forehead, and anyone within reach was liable to get a poke in the eye.

The band was due to leave Sourabaya at six o'clock the following morning, When Adeler arrived at the station he found Al already ensconced in the compartment. Unappeased, he told Al that he was no longer a member of the band, and ordered him off the train. When it steamed off up the line, Al was left sitting on the empty platform with one suitcase, a guitar and a banjo.

He made his way to a café which was the haunt of musicians in Sourabaya, where he was introduced to Dan Hopkins. Hopkins had been a company sergeant major in the Cameron Highlanders, stationed in Rawalpindi. He was also a good jazz drummer, and when a five-piece American Dixieland band had visited Rawalpindi in 1922, he had occasionally sat in with them. When the American drummer died of sunstroke, Hopkins had been invited to take his place. He bought himself out of the army, and became a jazz musician. Eventually he had formed his own band and toured Australia and the Far East, from Shanghai to Sourabaya—where he met up with Al. Al asked Hopkins if he could join his band, but since it was billed as the 'Dan Hopkins's Syncopated Five' there was no place for a sixth musician, and Hopkins had to turn him down. He did, however, find Al a room and a temporary job, as a waiter, with a French café owner.

Bowlly next turns up in Calcutta, towards the end of 1925. S. G. Vickers was then a European assistant in Thomas Cook's Calcutta office: 'I remember a young man who came into the office, in an obviously worried state of mind, to seek advice as to the possibility of working his passage to England. He said his name was Al Bowlly, and that he was stony broke. At the time the hot weather approach, 120 degrees, was upon us, and I was particularly struck by the fact that Al was wearing a very heavy leather jacket. He was in such a distressed state that, it being late afternoon, I stopped work and took him round to the chummery, which three of us shared. There I gave him tea, and, being of the same build, one of my white cotton suits and a clean outfit. The kindly treatment he met with caused him to break down completely, but he soon recovered and, using his banjo (the only item he carried with him), he treated us to a very pleasant interlude of song.'

In 1925, the Grand Hotel was the place to go for jazz in Calcutta. The proprietress, Mme Dubois, was determined to book the very best of the American bands that were then infiltrating all the capital cities of the Far East. Shanghai was the mecca for musicians from California, Europe and Russia, and the jazz king of Shanghai was Jimmy Lequime who led the band at the smartest dance-hall in the city, Mumm House. Lequime was Canadian. His band included a Philippino trombonist, Nick Ampier; an American drummer, Bill Houghton; and a Belgian sax-playing vocalist, Pete Harmon. The pianist was a White Russian refugee from the 1917 revolution—Monia Liter.

The word soon spread that this was the hottest band in Asia. Consequently Mme Dubois wrote to Jimmy Lequime and asked him to bring a large jazz orchestra to Calcutta to play at the Grand Hotel. He accepted the booking, and added three saxophone players to his Mumm House ensemble: Claude 'Sax' Maguire, Joe Speelman, and Vic Halek. Arriving at the Grand Hotel, the band soon made their mark. According to Speelman, 'After a few arranged numbers, the jute planters, who had plenty of money and drank prodigiously, would call for hotter and hotter music and the fun would become fast and furious.'

The band used to rehearse in the empty ballroom every morning for two or three hours. One day, Monia Liter recalls,

A young man came into the ballroom while we were rehearsing, and stood near the door, trying to catch the leader's eye. He was quite short, though powerfully built. What was really remarkable about his appearance was that he was dressed as a jockey, but, instead of a whip, he was carrying a banjo! I'd never seen a jockey with a banjo before! When we stopped playing, he came over and asked for the leader of the orchestra. Jimmy got off the stand, and spoke to him. I couldn't hear what they were saying. Eventually Jimmy turned back to the orchestra and said, 'Let's play a chorus of "Whispering".' And he said to the jockey, 'Get on the stand and see if you can busk the correct chords for this.' So he sat down, in his jockey clothes, and started to play. And he was very good! There and then Lequime said, 'You're in.' And that's how I first met Al Bowlly.

He *was* a good banjo player: and now, for the first time, recorded evidence of Al's musical skill becomes available. The manager of HMV's Dum Dum studios in Calcutta, hearing of the Lequime band's success, invited them to make a record. Monia Liter still has a copy of this record, now a rare collector's item. One side has 'Soho Blues', and the other has 'The House Where the Shutters are Green', which features a stunning banjo solo by Al Bowlly. If nothing else, it puts paid to the suggestion, made in later years, that Al's instrumental work was of no account. (It has even been said that his guitar was nothing more than a rubber-stringed prop, to give him something to do with his hands when he wasn't singing.) The truth is that as his singing career developed, he became less interested in the guitar and banjo. But the skill was always there—witness the fact that both Edgar Adeler and Jimmy Lequime first employed him in their bands as an instrumentalist, not as a singer.

There is a vocal chorus, sung by Pete Harmon, on the Calcutta record which provides a real clue as to why Al Bowlly's 'sweet' singing voice didn't appeal to 'hot' jazz addicts in the 1920s. Harmon uses his voice like a musical instrument—it's harsh, brash, noisy. And the Grand Hotel audiences loved him. Al Bowlly, however, was only allowed to sing in the café, which was in a side-street off Chowringhee, an annexe to the Grand Hotel. Here he sat in with the afternoon pianist, playing guitar and occasionally singing. Nobody was very impressed.

After four weeks at the Grand Hotel, Jimmy Lequime got an offer, which he accepted, to go to Singapore to play at the legendary Raffles Hotel. The band they were to replace was that of

Edgar Adeler and his Syncopators: the irony of this situation must have amused Bowlly as he headed for the bright lights of Singapore with his new employer.

'Raffles stands for all the fables of the exotic East,' said Somerset Maugham, who wrote many of his stories while staying there. Rudyard Kipling advised travellers to 'feed at Raffles when visiting Singapore'. Named after the founder of Singapore, Sir Stamford Raffles, by the early 1900s it had become world-famous for the social gaiety and colourful eccentricity of its guests, who thought nothing of downing ten bottles of gin before breakfast or shooting a tiger under the billiard table. To the musicians who had just arrived after a long and sweaty journey through Malaya, it was like stepping into a dreamworld. Monia Liter recalls:

> Our engagement there was supposed to be for two weeks, but we were so successful that the management of Raffles just wouldn't let us go. And so for a whole year the band played there. When I look back on our life in those days, it seems like a fairy-tale. We were treated like guests; each musician had a suite of rooms and individual servants. They even let us eat our meals in the grill room. We played a certain amount of jazz, but mostly it was music for dancing—foxtrots, tangos, paso dobles. The planters used to come in for tea-dances, and dinner-dances. They were always in full evening dress; you never saw anyone who wasn't properly dressed. And every Sunday night we would play a concert of symphonic music—Tchaikovsky, Debussy, Rachmaninov. Although I don't think Al Bowlly ever played in those concerts—that would have been his day off!

Monia Liter wrote most of the arrangements for the band, which kept him busy, while the other musicians enjoyed themselves: picnics at Lahore, golf, tennis, riding. Al Bowlly was the best horseman in the band. When the others pulled his leg about the shortness of his stirrup-leathers, he would remind them of his horse-riding experiences in Calcutta. He even claimed to have ridden the winner of the Calcutta Cup, though most listeners took this with a pinch of salt. He also loved to drive cars, although he didn't really know how to, and hadn't got a licence. But cars fascinated him, and he was so determined to become a good driver that he would frequently steal his friends' car-keys, and drive their vehicles to destruction.

In Singapore, Al Bowlly got his first real chance to make it as a singer. Peter Harmon left the band, gave up the music business, and returned to California to run a dogs' home. In his place, Lequime reluctantly allowed Al Bowlly to become the band's vocalist, and handed him the megaphone which was, in 1927, the only means of amplification available to a band singer. Al didn't like it very much. In later years he wrote:

> I am not over-fond of the megaphone, although I have found it necessary to use one from time to time. In the first place, it is apt to distort the voice; secondly, it is very 'directional', by which I mean that unless the megaphone is directed straight at a listener he will hear nothing but a muffled, wordless sound; thirdly, it hides the face and, whatever one might be tempted to say about this being an advantage, it is not, because it is impossible to express any sort of personality if one's face is replaced by a black gaping hole!

Despite these difficulties, Bowlly began to make an impact with the dancers at Raffles, particularly with the ladies. This growing relationship was never hampered by the kind of segregation between musicians and customers that was the rule in London's fashionable nightspots. In Singapore, everyone was very friendly. After all, as Monia Liter says, 'When you are young, it's nature's feeling that you want to have a companion to go out with, to hug and kiss etcetera. It's a natural thing. Without women, life becomes really very tedious and uninteresting. Al was always a very friendly person; he had a most generous nature, and if someone was generous in giving their love to him, he couldn't refuse . . .'

After a happy year in Singapore, the Lequime orchestra was disbanded. 'Sax' Maguire went to California, where he died of malaria and a pickled kidney. Bill Houghton went to South Africa to join a band led by sax-player Bert Ralton, one-time leader of the famous Savoy Havana Band. (He was subsequently shot in the leg on safari, and died through loss of blood.) Lequime gave up the music business and returned to Shanghai to make money. Al Bowlly headed for England but instead, in the spring of 1927, he turned up in Munich.

Germany in the 'twenties was jazz-crazy. Records from America, broadcasts from London, and musicians arriving from Africa and the Far East spread the word, and jazz became the style and spirit of the age. It's in the painting of George Grosz and Otto Dix, where grotesque saxophonists and leering black drummers ogle the jitterbugging flappers. It's in the poems of Walter Mehring, who absorbed the jazz slang as part of his language:

> I want to be down in Dixi
> Und cowboy rings
> Bei echten drinks!
> My darling girl schenk ein und mix sie!

It's in the songs of Bertolt Brecht and Kurt Weill who, half-satirically, half-romantically, used the sounds and rhythms of jazz to conjure up a fantasy world of adventure and romance. Curiously, they chose to locate their mythic El Dorado in those very same exotic places—Sourabaya, Mandalay, Cooch Behar—that had provided the real setting for Al's recent adventures.

At the Regina Palace Hotel in Munich, a new band was being formed under the leadership of Robert Gaden, a celebrated German violinist. He had enlisted the help of Edgar Adeler who, still en route to England, but now bandless, had recently arrived in Munich. While he and Gaden were scouting around for talent, Adeler was amazed to receive a letter from Singapore in which a contrite Al Bowlly apologized for his misdeeds and pleaded to be allowed to rejoin his old boss. Happy to bury the hatchet, Adeler persuaded Robert Gaden that Bowlly would be an asset to the band, and wrote to Al suggesting that he should leave Singapore immediately.

Al embarked for Marseilles, where Adeler assured him that he would find travelling instructions, and ten pounds to cover his expenses. But the money order went astray, and Al found himself in Marseilles penniless and jobless. The South African Consul loaned him his fare to Paris: from there he hitch-hiked to Munich where he presented himself, a week late and looking like a 'half-starved hobo', to a disbelieving Adeler. Somebody loaned him a dinner suit, and that same night Al Bowlly took his place in the Regina Palace Band. A truly international combination, the line-up included a German cellist (doubling tuba), an Italian saxophonist, an American trumpeter, a Hungarian drummer, and, from the East End of London, an eccentric 'hip' tenor saxophone player called Don Barrigo. 'At the first rehearsal,' recalls Barrigo, 'I smelt good music. Mario Benito, our lead saxophonist, had plenty of ideas—and modern at that. The long-haired stuff was played by Gaden and Joseph Redlich, who was a bit sticky on tuba. The guitarist Al Bowlly wasn't a great reader, but what he lacked in that respect, he made up for with his "ear". That boy had more harmony in his head than Mr Proust ever put down on paper! And sing?!!! Bowlly could bring the weeps on any dame, at any time, just by looking at them with his dark eyes and working his tonsils! He loved for me to play sax *obligatos* behind his vocals. Said it gave him ideas for his phrasing. I don't know how he could have improved on his phrasing, because it seemed perfect to us.'

Barrigo and Bowlly soon became good friends, and took rooms together in the Pension Max, which was in Maximilian Platz just round the corner from the Regina Palace. They shared a room on the third floor. Barrigo remembers that, among his few possessions, Al treasured a large crucifix which he hung on the wall over his bed.

Soon after his arrival in Munich, Al heard from Johannesburg that his father had died. Gaden offered to release him for as long as he wanted, but Al insisted that he would prefer to go on working. 'There was no laughing or fun on the stand that night,' says Don Barrigo. 'We all felt for Al, who was sentimental to a degree. The tears didn't cease falling from his eyes right through the evening session. I suggested to Gaden that we play no jazz on the programme that night, but Bowlly wouldn't hear of it. "Don't take any notice of me—play anything you like—I'll be with you," he said, tears running down his face like Niagara Falls. I think that some of my best choruses were played that night. I played and felt for Al, and my imagination went wild.'

Once established in Germany, Al was invited to work with other bands. He made records in Berlin for Arthur Briggs's Savoy Syncopators Orchestra—the first title, appropriately enough, was 'Song of the Wanderer'. He also recorded with George Carhart's New Yorkers' Jazz Orchestra, John Abriani's Six, and The Salon Symphonic Jazz Band of Fred Bird.

In 1928, the lure of the East beckoned once again. Adeler was offered a contract to lead a six-piece band at Firpo's Restaurant in Calcutta. Although it was still his ambition to reach London, he decided to accept the offer, which was a good one. He cabled the owner, Firpo, accepting the engagement, and suggesting that he might bring Al Bowlly with him as vocalist. Firpo's reply was short and sharp: 'Don't bring Bowlly'. Mystified, Adeler asked Al what lay behind this, and Al confessed that, on the last occasion he had played in Firpo's, an ugly brawl had developed between himself and the heavyweight boxing champion of India. The fight had started at the top of the stairs and ended at the bottom, with the Champ nursing a broken jaw.

Adeler took this explanation with a pinch of salt. Having personally come to blows with Al in Sourabaya, he reckoned him a very mediocre opponent—at least in a straight fight. But he also knew that there was an ugly side to Al's aggressive nature: in a hotel in Rhodesia, he had once gone into Al's room when the singer wasn't there and had seen, lying in his open suitcase, a brass knuckleduster.

Before Adeler left for Calcutta, he introduced Al to one of Berlin's top bandleaders, Fred Ross, who offered Al a job with his band at thirty-five marks a day. Adeler also made a last recording with Al, for the Homochord Company. The song they chose was Hoagy Carmichael's 'Muddy Water', and it was this record that provided Al with his passport to London.

In the spring of 1928, Len Fillis came to Berlin for a holiday. After leaving the Adeler band in Rhodesia, this brilliant young guitarist had made his way to London, and joined a new band at the Savoy Hotel, under the leadership of Fred Elizalde. In Berlin, Len Fillis renewed his friendship with Al, and when he returned to London, he took the Homochord record of 'Muddy Water' with him. He played it to 'Liz' (Elizalde), who was impressed, and cabled to Al, inviting him to come and join the band at the Savoy. The story goes that Elizalde sent Al twenty pounds for travelling expenses, which Al gambled away at the races, leaving him penniless once again, but that a friendly Munich businessman (his fairy godfather?) paid his overdue hotel bill, and bought him a first-class ticket to London. He arrived in July 1928.

Stomping at the Savoy

Built in 1889 on the site of the ancient home of the Earls of Savoy and Richmond, the Savoy was London's premier hotel. From the earliest days of modern dance music, the management had made it a policy to provide its rich and distinguished patrons with the best that money could buy. In 1920, Bert Ralton, who played banjo and saxophone, arrived in London with his New York Havana Band. By 1922 they had become the famous Savoy Havana Band, and the following year they were broadcasting regularly from the hotel.

The British Broadcasting Corporation may have favoured the Savoy as the place from which to inaugurate its regular outside broadcasts as much for its illustrious name as for the fact that the hotel was just around the corner from the BBC's new studio headquarters in Savoy Hill. Whatever the reason, dance music was to be broadcast from the Savoy with scarcely a break for the next twenty years. In December 1923, Reg Batten took over the Havana Band from Bert Ralton, and began to share the bandstand with the romantically named Savoy Orpheans, led by Debroy Somers. On both gramophone records and radio, the Savoy bands became a synonym for the very best. On 1 January 1928, a new name was added to an already distinguished list. It was Fred Elizalde and his Music.

Fred Elizalde was born in Manila in the Philippines in 1907, the son of wealthy and aristocratic Spanish parents who sent him to the United States to be educated and to study music. There, in the early 1920s, he heard the new jazz sounds that were sweeping across America: the trombone playing of Miff Mole, the saxophone playing of Frankie Trumbauer, the guitar playing of Eddie Lang, the trumpet playing of Red Nichols and of his own particular idol, Bix Beiderbecke. Elizalde was hooked. A talented musician—a fine pianist and a clever arranger—he had no doubt what his future was to be, and at the age of eighteen he was already leading his own dance band.

Back home in Manila Elizalde's parents were alarmed. A career as a jazz musician was hardly what they had planned for their son and heir. Hastily they despatched Fred and his younger brother Manuel (who played the saxophone) to Cambridge University in England, with the fervent hope that the sedate and cloistered atmosphere of those hallowed halls might cure them of this obsession. Alas, too late. By 1926, the year of Fred's arrival, the jazz virus had already crossed the Atlantic and was rampaging through the colleges. Before long Elizalde was in the thick of it. He formed a band called the Quinquaginta Club Ramblers which immediately became the most famous band in Cambridge. They even made records for Brunswick and HMV.

Inevitably Elizalde's fame spread, and by the autumn of 1927 he had been offered, and had accepted, the most coveted job in British dance music.

Even for the Savoy, the engagement of Fred Elizalde and his Music was an exciting and newsworthy event. The band was outstanding. Manuel had returned from the States with three star members of The California Ramblers, the band in whose honour Fred had named his Cambridge undergraduates. They were Bobby Davis, lead alto; Chelsea Quealey on trumpet; and Adrian Rollini on bass sax. The last-named was famous not only for his playing of that monstrously huge instrument, the bass saxophone, but also for such esoteric novelties as the hot fountain pen, a sort of sophisticated penny whistle, and the goofus, a weird contraption something like a harmonica with keys. The English musicians were Harry Hayes, a ridiculously young alto sax player (he was only sixteen years old at the time), Rex Owen on tenor sax, Norman Payne on trumpet and Ronnie Gubertini on drums. Al Bowlly's South African friend Len Fillis played banjo and guitar, and the singer was Dick Maxwell.

Even with this glittering array of talent, there could be no possible doubt about who was the star member of the orchestra; it was the handsome young Spaniard himself, immaculate in tails, seated at the grand piano. Fred Elizalde was no mere front man;

as an arranger he was already considered a leader among those who were exploring new and exciting ways of scoring music for the modern dance band, and as a pianist he was considered by many to be the best outside America. Brunswick had just released a record featuring two of his piano solos, 'By The Waters Of Minnetonka' and 'Pianotrope', an original composition. The *Melody Maker* reviewer produced a panegyric in which the word 'genius' was much bandied about. Of 'Pianotrope' he wrote: 'The themes are hauntingly tuneful and the treatment given them —in some parts dead straight, in others with the hottest of modern dance rhythms—is based on a harmony which, while being very modern, is still easily understandable.'

Opening night at the Savoy was a social event. With his dark good looks, his assured and elegant manner, Elizalde was already the darling of London society. Stanley Jackson, a show business reporter, wrote about it some time later: 'No expense was spared to present Elizalde's orchestra as a symbol of super-sophisticated entertainment. The musicians sat on a platform turret like a mediaeval castle and painted in red, gold and silver.' It was said that Mrs Louis Oppenheimer gave a dinner party for a hundred and twenty guests and presented Elizalde with laurel leaves.

Shortly after the band opened, Adrian Rollini had to return to America to visit his sick father, and to replace him Elizalde engaged 'Tiny' Stock on string bass and tuba and added George Hurley on violin. Rollini soon returned, but Hurley and Stock were kept on, thus making the band twelve strong. Dick Maxwell, the singer, was replaced by another, Eddie Sheldon.

The Savoy management, however, was becoming somewhat dissatisfied with its glamorous new bandleader. In fact, they were beginning to doubt the wisdom of having engaged him at all. The trouble was that Elizalde, interested only in the music he loved, insisted on playing jazz. The patrons of the Savoy restaurant, staid, conventional and accustomed to getting their own way, complained that his tempos were impossible to dance to— either frantically fast or else turgidly slow; also that he absolutely refused to play waltzes! Worse still, he was fond of featuring his own symphonic compositions (the best known of which was called 'The Heart Of A Nigger'!) in which long *rubato* passages, exciting *accelerandos* and mournful *rallentandos* would leave the dancers stranded in mid-floor until some recognizable dance tempo reasserted itself.

There was trouble, too, about the band's BBC broadcasts, which had started immediately upon their arrival at the Savoy. Listeners were writing in to complain that they couldn't recognize their favourite tunes. Elizalde haughtily ignored them. In an interview he declared: 'I am not definitely opposed to melody, but to me it is an entirely secondary consideration as far as dance music is concerned.' The BBC grumbled, the Savoy management pleaded; Elizalde grudgingly made a few concessions to popular taste. He continued to be dissatisfied with his singer. Eddie Sheldon had already replaced Dick Maxwell, and then in July, Elizalde having heard and liked the records which Len Fillis had played him, Sheldon was replaced by Al Bowlly.

When Al arrived in London, in 1928, it must have seemed like a dream come true. At last, here he was at the very heart of the British Empire. The sights and sounds of the great city astonished and excited him. The West End, he decided, was his spiritual home. And there was music, music everywhere. Besides the Savoy there were the other great hotels, each with its famous band. The Cecil, where Jack Payne played; the Carlton with Ben Davis's Band, The Piccadilly with Al Starita, and the Mayfair with Ambrose. There were the smart clubs and restaurants: Ciro's, The Embassy, the Kit-Kat where Arthur Rosebury was playing. Chez Henri with Charlie Kunz, The Café Royal, Romano's, Frascati's, and dozens more. And there were the night-clubs where good jazz was played, and where the West End musicians went after hours to sit in with the band or just to relax: The Silver Slipper, The Bag O'Nails, The Hambone and The Gargoyle.

There was scarcely time for Bowlly to meet his new boss and get his bearings in this vast and bewildering city before the Savoy engagement ended for the summer break, and Elizalde took the band off for a six-week gig on the Continent. There had been time, however, for Al to make his first record with the band for Brunswick. *Melody Maker* greeted it warmly:

Al Bowlly is a real find. He has an alluring voice and favours the sweet *legato* rhythm style of rendering: but when he does sing 'hot'—oh boy! With the Elizalde band, he has just made his first records in this country, the titles being 'Just Imagine', 'Wherever You Are' and 'After My Laughter Came Tears'. The band go to Paris next week, to play at the Restaurant des Ambassadeurs in the Champs Elysée, where they go in for the best of everything and charge appropriate prices to their clients.

For the prestigious Paris engagement (they were following such bands as Paul Whiteman and Fred Waring's Pennsylvanians), Elizalde again augmented the band. Another raid on the California Ramblers had captured their pianist, Jack Rusin. George Hurley was joined by two more violinists, Len Lee and Ben Frankel, nicknamed 'Winkle', who later, as a composer, was to become one of the most distinguished figures in British contemporary music. George Smith from Jack Hylton's Kit-Kat band joined the saxophone section, Nobby Knight, on trumpet, joined the brass, and Mario Lorenzi, who played jazz on the harp and was already famous in the music halls, completed the ensemble.

After Paris the band held a short engagement in Ostend and, on 1 October 1928, Elizalde returned to the Savoy, where Reg Batten's Savoy Orpheans and Al Collins's Orchestra from Claridge's had been filling in for him. Fred Elizalde was now an international celebrity and the hotel welcomed him back with open arms. He increased the band's number to eighteen by adding Jack Miranda on alto sax, and his was now the only dance band in the hotel. Since it was impossible for them to play continuously throughout all the hours of dancing at the Savoy (tea-dancing was a recreation enthusiastically indulged in by the smart clientele), Elizalde took to splitting the band in two at certain times. One combination was led by Bobby Davis on alto sax and included Al Bowlly on banjo. They played the melodic music favoured by the hotel's older patrons and even managed a few waltzes. The other was led by Adrian Rollini with his bass sax and played uncompromising hot jazz. For recording purposes this band was called 'Fred Elizalde's Rhythmicians' and Al recorded two titles with them: 'After The Sun Kissed The World Goodbye' and 'If Anything Happened To You'.

Melody Maker rejoiced in Elizalde's return to the Savoy, and proclaimed it 'a triumph for "hot" music in its most modern form'. It pointed gleefully to the fact that although 'the Grannies' had foretold nothing but disaster for such a music policy, their gloomy predictions had proved false. In spite of complaints 'from the older and more regular of the Savoy's patrons', there had to be, if there was not already, 'a distinct demand for dance music of the more advanced and stylish kind'. But *Melody Maker*'s crystal ball seems to have been somewhat clouded on this occasion, as events were soon to prove.

Al had now settled down as a regular member of the band. With his arrival Elizalde's dissatisfied chopping and changing of band singers had ceased. The boss was clearly happy with the new boy. He got along well enough with his fellow musicians, but one doubts that they had much time for the brash and easy-going South African who had joined them. Jazz musicians have always been notoriously indifferent to the singers in their midst, and there is no reason to believe that Fred Elizalde's men were exceptional in that regard. The customers liked him, however, especially the ladies, who responded to his dazzling smile and his sweetly romantic crooning.

The band resumed their broadcasting, but Elizalde's relationship with the BBC continued to deteriorate. Again and again the Corporation passed on to him the complaints of listeners and adjured him to include more melodic items in his programmes. He refused. The band would play the music of his choosing and nothing else. If he couldn't bring his brand of modern jazz to the people of Britain, then he would prefer not to broadcast at all. The BBC chose the latter alternative. On 28 February 1929, late-night dance music from the Savoy came to an end.

This was a bitter blow, not only for Al Bowlly, but also for the hotel. The popularity of radio had been increasing rapidly over the past two years; by 1929, the BBC could claim no less than ten million listeners. The Savoy was not pleased. The loss of broadcasting meant a loss of prestige.

On 29 April, Elizalde undertook a two-week engagement on

the stage of the London Palladium. At that time bands were not the attraction in the music halls that they were to become in the mid-1930s. They did not occupy the exalted top-of-the-bill position, nor were they the principal drawing card in the company. Few had attempted the difficult move from bandstand to theatre stage. In 1919, the Original Dixieland Jazz Band had appeared at the London Hippodrome (and had been fired because the star, George Robey, feared that they were stealing his thunder), and in 1923 Paul Whiteman had brought his famous orchestra from America to appear in the same theatre. The following year, Jack Hylton, emulating Whiteman, decided that henceforth the stage was to be his natural habitat. He appeared at the Alhambra and so set the standard for musical showmanship for the next decade. But it was not until 1931, when Harry Roy opened the new RKO theatre in Leicester Square, that dance bands began to take their theatre appearances seriously.

There were some new faces in the band Elizalde took to the Palladium. More Americans had found seats in the front line. Arthur Rollini, Adrian's brother, was on tenor sax, Max Farley on saxophone and flute, and Fud Livingston, already a legendary name among jazz clarinettists, had replaced young Harry Hayes. The band was now twenty-three strong, and in addition, two dancers, Jean Barry and Dave Fitzgibbons, were featured. The fans complained that because of the amount of space required by the dancers, the band had been set too far back on the stage, causing the ensemble to sound thin and the subtlety of much of the solo playing to be lost.

All agreed, however, that the stage setting, consisting of draperies and pillars with floral decorations, was beautiful. Norman Payne, playing trumpet with the band, remembers one night at the Palladium when one of those pillars broke loose from its moorings and hit Al Bowlly smartly on the head, knocking him out cold. Norman suspects that Al 'may have been putting on a bit of an act', and certainly the singer would not have been slow to see the dramatic possibilities in such a mishap. Anyway, he recovered soon enough and continued the performance, none the worse for the experience.

Melody Maker devoted a good deal of space to a review of

Elizalde's Palladium appearance, and paid particular tribute to the presentation:

> The moment that supplied the biggest thrill and the pleasantest recollection was the playing of 'Lover Come Back To Me'—a melody foxtrot, in which the band excelled to such an extent as to receive almost unprecedented eulogies from rhythm enthusiasts, the lay press music critics, and Sir Thomas Beecham himself. The harmonized vocal effects by the whole band behind Al Bowlly's vocal chorus were really electric. Seldom, if ever, has such perfect balance and intonation been heard from a dance band, and the machine-like raising and lowering of twenty or more megaphones was the only piece of obviously attempted and successful showmanship indulged in.

Al Bowlly, the vocalist in the band, who was well featured, has been freely criticized for a certain measure of untutored enunciation and a tendency for his high notes to lack pitch. This is not really justified by the facts, and against any defects, one can put a nice style which, while it is not 'hot', is characteristically rhythmic.

The reviewer's sour comment about Al's 'untutored enunciation' and the dubious pitch of his high notes referred, of course, to what had been heard of him on the Savoy broadcasts and on the few records he had made. Al had recorded only two titles with Elizalde: 'If I Had You' and 'I'm Sorry Sally'. He had also recorded with a band led by Van Phillips, a brilliant American arranger, who had been responsible for many of the successful Jack Hylton scores. The song Al had sung was 'Sometimes', and one reviewer had this to say about the record:

> Al Bowlly sounds vile when broadcast. There is no other word for it. He never seems to be in pitch and appears to have a mouth full of hot plums. I don't know whether it is because of the conditions—he may have to shout to reach the mike or it may be the effect of the megaphone he uses—but there it is, and consequently everyone who had heard him only via the radio says he's a rotten vocalist. He's not. He's a wonderful singer, and if you want to prove it for yourself hear him on this record.

It should be remembered that all this happened at a time when the public address system, the stand microphone which amplifies the singer's voice for the benefit of his audience in dance hall or theatre, had yet to make its appearance. Crooners were still using the megaphone, that device borrowed from public orators and rowing-eight coxswains. Even on recordings and broadcasts, a crooner would have to sing through his megaphone and into the microphone in order to make himself heard above the sound of the orchestra. Commenting on the 'faraway sound' of his voice on those early recordings, Al had this to say: 'Yes indeed—singers like me had to stand to one side, or back to the band and hope to reach the recording mike with something! It was the band first and all the time.'

Some years later, when the singer's microphone had replaced the megaphone and Al had mastered it, he was to write eloquently on the subject of microphone technique for the benefit of all aspiring vocalists:

> Many singers, unless they have had years of training and intensive practice, find that the top notes of their chest register are round and clear but of little volume. Any endeavour to make them strong enough for concert-hall purposes forces them beyond the power of the vocal chords, with consequent loss of their best and only virtue—sweetness.
>
> The microphone, however, with its magic, makes those soft notes as loud as necessary. And, of course, this applies to the whole range of the voice. Forcing is wholly unnecessary, and every effort can be concentrated on the quality of the voice rather than the quantity. An entirely different voice-quality is the result . . . Without a microphone, crooning is no longer characteristic, although I have tried singing without artificial aid in large theatres and so on, and been assured that I was audible at the back of the hall. Nevertheless, the voice loses that intimacy which is so essential a part of this kind of singing.

During April and May, Al made some records with other bands. He recorded two titles with Percival Mackey, a pianist band leader, and his concert orchestra: 'When The Lilacs Bloom

Again' and 'Up In The Clouds'. He also joined his old friend Len Fillis who was playing the Hawaiian guitar and recording under the title of Linn Milford and his Hawaiian Players and Singers. (Conflicting contracts often made it advisable for musicians to do their extra-mural recording under pretty outlandish pseudonyms.) For Len, Al recorded a song called 'Honeymoon Chimes'.

Fred Elizalde continued to play at the Savoy, and the band's reputation with the real dance music fans, that dedicated group whose bible was the *Melody Maker*, was steadily growing. When, in November, *Melody Maker* conducted a poll to decide its readers' most popular band, Fred Elizalde and his Music was voted number one. Next came Ambrose and his Mayfair Hotel Orchestra, and then Jack Payne and his newly formed BBC Dance Orchestra.

At the Savoy, the band was now sharing the night's work with Geraldo and his Gaucho Tango Orchestra; the same Geraldo who would later lead a famous dance band, but who was at that time masquerading as a moustachioed Latin American cowboy, resplendent in embroidered wide-sleeved shirt and riding boots. While Elizalde's quarrels with the hotel's management grew more and more bitter, his fame and popularity among the jazz enthusiasts of Europe continued to increase. In June, three thousand fans turned up from Denmark, France and Belgium for a concert at the Shepherd's Bush Pavilion. Two thousand more local fans had to be turned away at the door.

The Savoy contract ended on 31 July. It was not renewed. Elizalde's comment:

> No, I didn't fire the hotel, the hotel fired me. I have received a wonderful letter from the directors thanking me for, as they put it, all I have done, and stating that in their opinion the band has been a complete success. All of which doesn't alter the fact that the contract hasn't been renewed. The reason, I understand, is that the directors think a change is good for everybody. Of course I know that in the same way as the great majority of the patrons of the hotel have thoroughly enjoyed the band—they have been kind enough to tell me so—there is a handful of

others more elderly and not so up-to-date in their appreciation of dance music, whom it has not pleased to the same extent.

He was replaced by Al Collins and his Orchestra from the Savoy's sister hotel, the Berkeley. Collins's was a 'house band', disciplined and conventional. They would play whatever the Savoy asked of them, and cause no trouble.

Defiantly, Elizalde took his band on a tour of Scotland and the north of England. The seventeen musicians included the Americans Adrian and Arthur Rollini, Bobby Davis and Max Farley. Al Bowlly was the singer and guitarist. The tour was a fiasco, as Albert McCarthy has noted in his book, *The Dance Band Era*:

> By all accounts Elizalde was not by nature a business man, nor, it would seem, a very far-sighted individual, for after leaving the Savoy, he led the band on a tour of Northern and Scottish music halls which, predictably, proved to be disastrous. The modern arrangements were met with incomprehension or downright hostility by the audiences; the greatest humiliation was incurred at Edinburgh, where the band was forced to give way to the resident pit orchestra. One report—probably apocryphal—claims that part of their trouble in Scotland stemmed from their inability to play reels!

Discouraged and bitter, and having spent a great deal of his own money in the effort to keep the band together, Elizalde returned to London. At Elstree Studios he recorded the music for a film starring Pola Negri, and began negotiations for the band to return to the Savoy. Unfortunately the Ministry of Labour refused to renew the work permits for the Rollini brothers, Max Farley and Bobby Davis; and, since the Savoy directors were making the deal contingent upon a personal appearance of the Americans, it fell through.

On Christmas Eve 1929, Elizalde paid off his musicians and disbanded. The Americans went home to resume their interrupted careers, the Rollinis and Fud Livingston in particular to make important contributions to the development of modern jazz. Elizalde himself left for Paris. He returned to England from time to time—once to conduct some of his own music from the pit of the Duchess Theatre for a show called *The Intimate Revue*, and on another occasion to record some of his own inimitable piano solos for Decca.

But his interest in jazz was waning; unresponsive audiences and hostile managements had blunted the edge of his enthusiasm. He was drawn more and more towards classical music, and studied for a while with Maurice Ravel. In 1933 he left Paris for Madrid, where he studied with the great Spanish composer Manuel de Falla. When civil war broke out in Spain in 1936, he fought on Franco's side, and in 1939 he went home to the Philippines. He returned to England in 1951, for the Festival of Britain, when he conducted at Royal Festival Hall.

It is sad that this brilliant musician, whose appearance on the jazz scene had seemed to promise so much for British dance music, did not stay long enough to fulfil that promise. The simple fact is that his ideas were ahead of the times, and it would be many years before British audiences would be ready to respond to the kind of music that he had attempted to introduce during his brief but fascinating stay at the Savoy.

This turn of events was sadder still for Al Bowlly who, a little more than eighteen months after his arrival in England, suddenly found himself without a steady job.

Brother, Can You Spare a Dime?

1930 was to be a bad year for Al Bowlly. It was, let's face it, a bad year for most people. The 'twenties, that frivolous decade, had ended messily and melodramatically with the Wall Street Crash, and already its aftermath, the Great American Depression, was beginning to have a chilling effect on British life. By 1932 there would be three million unemployed.

True, the West End seemed scarcely to miss a beat of four-four time—the hotels, restaurants and smart clubs all continued to flourish—but the winds were blowing decidedly colder, and it was no time to be without a steady income. Especially if you were Al Bowlly, who spent it when he had it, loaned it or gave it away when he could afford it, and never spared a thought for rainy days ahead. On the day Fred Elizalde paid off his band, Al's bank balance was seventeen pounds.

He hadn't been in England long enough to build a solid reputation, and dance-band crooners were still far from becoming the indispensable assets that the demands of a hero-worshipping radio audience would make them a couple of years hence. In many cases, the singer was still an anonymous voice on gramophone records, his (or her) presence acknowledged on the label only by the legend 'with vocal refrain'. They were still banjoists, saxophone players, pianists and drummers first, crooners second; bathtub singers with patience enough to learn the words of a popular song, and nerve enough to stand up in front of the band and bawl an occasional chorus through a megaphone. Those who came closest to being singers, first and foremost, were Cavan O'Connor with Percival Mackey's band; Les Allan with Pete Mandell; Harry Shalson with Al Starita; Pat O'Malley with Jack Hylton; Billy Scott-Coomber with Jack Payne; Val Rosing with Billy Cotton; and Sam Browne, who was just beginning to make himself heard with Ambrose.

Al did the rounds of the agents and the managers, but found no joy anywhere. Nobody needed a singer, not even one who also played useful rhythm guitar and banjo. Once more, his old friend Len Fillis came to the rescue. Len, who had been working at the Piccadilly Hotel with a band led by Al Starita, since leaving Elizalde, had thought up a four-handed act for the music halls which he called The Blue Boys. It consisted of himself, Al Starita (an American who was having labour-permit difficulties), Edgar Adeler, that other South African with whom Al had worked on the Continent, and Al himself. It seems that Len Fillis had discovered that Al was no mere vocalist. He was also quite a fair pianist, and, as if that wasn't enough accomplishment for one man, he was a good dancer! Thus the act could present Al and Edgar Adeler playing two pianos and doing what one reviewer described as 'some novel vocalising', Len Fillis playing banjo and guitar, Al Starita with his bass and C-melody saxophones and his clarinet—and Al Bowlly dancing.

D. J. Clark, a theatre proprietor was a friend of Edgar Adeler's father, and so on 20 January The Blue Boys opened at one of his theatres, the Argyle, in Birkenhead. The act was a bit raw and not a howling success, but the dance-band fans welcomed two of their favourites, Len Fillis and Al Starita, while there was no doubt that it was the two unknowns, Edgar Adeler and Al Bowlly, who were providing whatever showmanship the act displayed.

Success came in the form of a contract to appear with Harry Gordon, the Scottish comedian, for a summer season in Aberdeen at the handsome fee of £120 a week. But there was friction between the volatile Al Bowlly and the equally explosive Italian-American Al Starita. At a one-night stand in Aldershot, Len Fillis and Edgar Adeler burst into one of the dressing rooms to find Al Starita with a soda syphon raised above Al Bowlly's head, and the latter with a knife at Starita's throat. Len and Edgar managed to separate them, but that was the end of The Blue Boys. They cancelled the contract with Harry Gordon, and Al was back on the bread line.

However, all was not completely lost. Len Fillis, virtuoso of all the fretted instruments, had got himself some nice recording dates with a small band. Music with a Polynesian flavour was much in demand in the early 'thirties, and songs like 'Blue Pacific Moonlight' and 'Aloha Oe' were all the rage. Len was master of the Hawaiian guitar, an instrument played flat across the knees, which, when stopped by a steel bar, emitted long swooping *glissandi*, conjuring up, for some, a vision of coconut palms, azure skies, and white-crested waves breaking gently upon golden sands. Others it just made seasick.

Fillis recorded his band under a variety of names and on a variety of record labels. For Regal he had been recording for some time as Linn Milford and his Hawaiian Singers; for Dominion, they became The Honolulu Serenaders; and for the Celebrity label, The Hawaiian Octet. For Piccadilly, he was known as Earl Melville and his Hawaiians; for Decca, he could choose from The Hawaiian Serenaders, The Palm Beach Hawaiians or The Phantom Players. For Broadcast Records, he was Ferrachini's Hawaiian Band. The Hawaiian Serenaders also recorded for the Victory Label, a seven-inch disc made exclusively for Woolworth's, where it sold for that store's maximum price of sixpence.

Throughout 1930, Al recorded sixty or more titles with Len Fillis in one or another of his many disguises. All the same, the sessions, no more than one a month and modestly paid (three pounds maximum for a morning's work), must have done little to keep the wolf from the door.

There were other recording sessions, mostly with house bands, such as Jay Wilbur at Crystallate and Harry Hudson at Edison Bell. For Jay Wilbur's Aldwych Players, Al recorded more songs for Woolworth's Victory label, among them 'On the Sunny Side of the Street' and 'Dancing with Tears in my Eyes'. For Harry Hudson, masquerading as The Radio Melody Boys and The Blue Jays, he sang duets with Les Allan, songs like 'My Sunshine Came On A Rainy Day' and 'Underneath The Spanish Stars'. He even had a session with Marius B. Winter, the first bandleader to broadcast, way back in March 1923, from Marconi House in London. For Winter, Al sang 'Roamin' Thru' The Roses' and 'Never Swat A Fly'.

Al had one last asset to exploit during that lean year—he could sing in Afrikaans. British recording companies were eager to export and South Africa, a rapidly expanding outpost of the Empire, was high on their list of overseas markets. Brian Rust's discography reveals that Al Bowlly first recorded an Afrikaans-language record with a piano accompaniment by Gideon Fagan on 10 June 1930. That session was to lead to one of the most important encounters of Bowlly's life—with Ray Noble, HMV's new Director of Light Music. The story of their meeting is told by Ray Noble himself in a later chapter; suffice it to say here that from Al Bowlly's point of view it could hardly have been more momentous.

On 30 June Al did a test session with Noble and a small orchestra and sang his Afrikaans songs. That fence having successfully been taken, two weeks later he was offered a regular session. He sang *Banditlied* ('The Prisoner's Song'), and *Kleine Maat* ('Little Pal').

But this was all long before Ray Noble had put his New Mayfair Orchestra firmly on the recording map, and meanwhile Al was down to his last three pounds and his landlady was clamouring for the rent.

Al was desperate. Surely there must be some way he could pick up a few pounds? London's streets were then full of buskers. Some survive to this day, but in 1930 they were everywhere. Every theatre and cinema queue had its banjo player, its paper tearer, its soft-shoe dancer, its virtuoso of the musical spoons, or its queenly ballad singer, her hand cupped soulfully over her ear. And what Londoner of that time will ever forget the sad little groups of unemployed Welsh miners, shuffling along the gutters of West End streets (the police required them to keep moving), singing their defiant songs of the Rhondda in plangent harmony?

Al had watched the buskers often, and, when times were good, had added many a half-crown to the meagre display of copper in old cloth caps. He reviewed his assets: a guitar, a banjo, a singing voice and three quid. Well, if the man in the grand hotel and the smart restaurant didn't want him, perhaps the man in the street might. Without hesitating, he put his guitar under his arm, pulled his hat down over his eyes and sallied forth. He wandered the West End streets looking for a good pitch. Theatre and cinema queues were promising, and so were the entrances to Underground stations. He waited with the other buskers, and when his turn came placed his hat at his feet, slung his guitar into position and sang his favourite songs. Nobody recognized him, and nobody paid him any more attention than they did the paper tearers and the virtuosi of the spoons. When, at the end of a week, he totted up his 'take', he had earned the princely sum of two pounds and seventeen shillings.

Meanwhile, elsewhere in London, an American trumpet-playing bandleader had just arrived to fulfil an eight-week engagement at the Café de Paris. Roy Fox lived in Beverly Hills. He had just given up the band he had been leading at the Cocoanut Grove in Hollywood, because he had been offered the job of Head of the Music Production Department at Twentieth Century-Fox Films. Then he had received the cable offering the Café de Paris engagement. Seeking advice, he consulted Abe Lyman who had already visited London and played with his band at the Kit-Kat. Abe painted a glamorous picture of the Café de Paris ('nothing but royalty—the Prince of Wales, the Duke of Kent, they dance there all the time'), and urged Roy to get leave from the studio and go.

Within days Roy Fox and his band were aboard the SS *Majestic* and sailing for England. Fox recalls: 'I got together a band of studio musicians. We hadn't even a chance to rehearse; we were going to do that on the *Majestic*. And I thought, although I'm a very bad sailor, this ship is so large, there should be no chance of becoming seasick. Well, it was such a rough voyage that I was sick all the way over. And so was the band.'

Roy Fox and his unrehearsed band opened at the Café de Paris and nobody was impressed, especially since he followed his compatriot Hal Kemp on to the bandstand, whose slick and jazzy ten-piece band had included the great trumpeter, Bunny Berigan.

Fortunately, Edward Lewis, who had just launched the Decca Record Company and was eager to compete with the long established His Master's Voice, had spotted a potential star in the tall and handsome American. He offered him a recording contract provided he would stay in England when the Café de Paris engagement ended and form an all-British band. Fox, due to return to his job at the film studios in Hollywood, hesitated and then agreed. He later recalled: 'I thought that it would be nice to stay over in Europe for a while, and finally they offered me such a good deal that I gave up my job at Fox.'

Roy Fox, a stranger in a strange land, needed somebody to help him put the band together. He engaged Bill Harty, the dapper little drummer who had already made himself something of an *eminence grise* behind Ray Noble at HMV. Nat Gonella called Harty 'Diplomatic Bill': 'Because he was the brains behind everything, you see? And you could always reckon if he was talking to you that there was an undercurrent somewhere.' Fox also recruited Nat Gonella and Sid Buckman on trumpets, Joe Ferrie on trombone, Ernest Ritte on alto saxophone and Lew Stone as the pianist and arranger.

Soon after Fox had formed his band he learned that a new restaurant, The Monseigneur, was shortly to open in Jermyn Street and was shopping for a band. They auditioned for the job and got it. 'It meant,' said Roy, 'that I had to add a vocalist to the band. So I talked it over with Lew Stone and Bill Harty and one or two of the boys, because naturally I didn't know one musician from another over here.'

'I said, what about a vocalist? And they said, "We know the very person." And I said, well, who's that? "Well," they said. "It's a guy by the name of Al Bowlly." I said, "Well where is he? When can I hear him?" And they said, "Well unfortunately he's entertaining the theatre queues. But he's really terrific!" Well I didn't know about busking and all that, so I said, "What do you mean? What's he doing that for? And how can he be so terrific if he's singing for theatre queues?" '

If this poised and confident musician from Hollywood had not already suspected that his English counterparts were just a little eccentric, this baffling conversation must surely have confirmed him in that view. Bill Harty, aided and abetted by the others, argued so convincingly and praised Al Bowlly's gifts so lavishly that Roy finally agreed to audition him. Bill tracked him down and brought him to meet Roy Fox in an office in Coventry Street. The song he sang was, appropriately enough, 'Please'. 'He sang a few notes', remembers Roy, 'and I knew immediately that that was the boy I wanted for my vocalist.'

There is a story, often told but probably untrue, that Al was so desperate to impress his potential boss that after the audition he insisted on taking Roy Fox and his wife to a nearby restaurant, where he spent his last three pounds on a slap-up lunch. After lunch, the story goes, Al approached the restaurant bandleader, and after a hurried consultation with the pianist, leapt on to the bandstand and sang a couple of numbers, whereupon all Roy Fox's remaining doubts were dissipated, and he said, simply: 'Okay, you get the job.'

Roy Fox does recall, however, that never in his life had he seen anybody so happy to get a job. 'He was absolutely dead broke. So I'll never forget when I presented him with his first pay cheque, he said, "Boss...". He always used to call me Boss. [Fox thought it had something to do with Al's being born in South Africa.] "Boss," he said, "I'd like to take you to lunch and spend part of it on you." So he took me to a little Italian restaurant in Soho, and he ordered a meal. There was a chicken course among others, during which I heard a strange noise coming from Al—he was chewing the chicken bones! He said, "That's the best part of the chicken, Boss. Look at my teeth." And it's true, he did have the most marvellous strong white teeth. I'll never forget that lunch.'

Roy Fox made his first records for Decca on 7 January 1931. Al sang on two of the titles: 'Memories Of You' and 'Thank Your Father'. The band recorded again on the 16th, the 24th and 28th, when Al sang 'Can't We Be Friends', 'Wedding Bells Are Ringing For Sally', 'The Missouri Waltz', 'Lady Play Your Mandoline', 'Hurt', 'Writing A Letter To You', and 'A Peach Of A Pair'.

The Great Depression was tightening its grip. In New York there were soup kitchens in Times Square, and in London the dole queues lengthened. Y. P. Harburg and Jay Gorney wrote a song which Sigmund Spaeth, the American musicologist said 'came nearest to expressing the spirit of the day'. The song was called 'Brother, Can You Spare A Dime?', Al Bowlly was to sing it, and it was to become his theme song: 'Say, don't you remember, they called me Al? It was Al all the time.' But in January 1931, the song did not express his mood. He was a happy man; he had a steady job with a marvellous band, and The Monseigneur was due to open its doors in May. The bad times were over, and the best was yet to come.

The Magic Circle

The big-time musicians of the 'thirties were those who played nightly in London's West End hotels, restaurants and exclusive clubs, with bands led by such as Ambrose, Lew Stone, Sidney Lipton, Jack Jackson and Carroll Gibbons; at the BBC with Jack Payne; or on tour with Jack Hylton. But the true élite among dance-band musicians were the session men; those who, besides holding down a steady job with one or other of the famous-name bands, were also in demand in the studios for making records, for broadcasting and for accompanying the stars of the new all-talking, all-singing, all-dancing films that were made at Elstree, Twickenham and Islington, and later at Denham and Pinewood.

To be a session musician you needed two qualifications: a flawless technique and impeccable sight-reading ability. Additionally, you had to be punctual, sober, and as disciplined as a Coldstream Guardsman. Recording sessions were expensive and time was of the essence. If a session was called for 10 am the musical director's baton would descend at thirty seconds past the hour, and any playing of wrong notes, which led to additional 'takes', was simply not to be tolerated.

Recording sessions took place in the mornings and afternoons (the nights belonged to the West End bandleaders) and were three hours long, during which it was expected that four titles would be recorded. This was long before the electronic marvels of magnetic tape and twenty-four track stereo; recordings were made on wax masters revolving on a turntable at seventy-eight revolutions a minute. When the red light glowed, the recording began, and continued for the more or less three minutes of its duration. If a saxophone player blew a wrong note, if a trumpeter hit a clinker or noisily dropped a mute, the take was ruined and the whole process had to begin all over again. Hence the ultra-efficiency of the session boys.

They were required, of course, to give priority to the broadcasting and recording dates set up by their regular bands, but outside of those they were free to accept as much freelance work as time allowed. Apart from large string sections which were usually recruited from established orchestras like the London Symphony or the Royal Philharmonic, there were probably no more than one hundred of these pampered virtuosi. Other musicians complained bitterly that a mere handful were claiming all the session work (Nat Gonella called it 'a magic circle', impossible to penetrate), but musical directors, a conservative breed, preferred to stick to the players whose work they knew well and felt they could trust.

Principal contractors for this lucrative daytime work were the musical directors of the house bands maintained by all important recording companies. Harry Hudson reigned at Edison Bell, Bert Firman at Zonophone, and Jay Wilbur's band recorded for the Crystallate Company on the Imperial and Eclipse labels. But the most coveted sessions of all, the musician's equivalent of being selected to play Test cricket for England, were with the house band at HMV, under the musical directorship of Ray Noble.

Ray Noble was born in Brighton in 1907, and studied classical piano from the age of ten. As a schoolboy, he went to the Wimbledon Palais de Danse, and heard the pianist play Zez Confrey's flashily syncopated and fiendishly difficult composition, 'Kitten On The Keys'. Absolutely knocked out by it, he found a copy of the music, locked himself in his front parlour and sat at the piano until he had mastered it. From that moment on he abandoned the classics; dance music was all he could think of. He formed a small group of local lads and played for dances around South London. In 1927, he won a competition for arrangers organized by *Melody Maker* (his winning score was recorded by Bert Firman on Zonophone), and joined the music publishing firm of Lawrence Wright in the Charing Cross Road as a staff arranger. Ray Noble continues the story: 'Dance-band arrangers were a new thing then. You had theatrical arrangers, but now the dance bands were becoming important because the BBC's outside broadcasts were getting a tremendous amount of attention. I did arrangements for practically every band in town. And from Lawrence Wright I went to the BBC to arrange for Jack Payne who had the house orchestra there.'

In July 1929, Carroll Gibbons, then leading the Orpheans at the Savoy and working as Light Music Director for HMV, was offered a contract with MGM in Hollywood. He called Noble and offered him the HMV job. Noble was both flattered and scared, and said he didn't think he could do it. Carroll Gibbons replied, 'Nothing like trying it to see if you can.'

He could. Soon the records he made with The New Mayfair Orchestra were as popular with the public as any made by the big-name bands. The reason is not hard to find. Ray Noble was a perfectionist. Every aspect of his work—the playing, the intonation, the orchestral balance—was given the utmost attention. He would endlessly rehearse details of each score, and no record was released until he was absolutely satisfied that no further improvements could be made.

At HMV, the privilege of recording the best of the new songs always went to the two star bands under contract to the company, those of Ambrose and Jack Hylton. The function of the house band was to fill in the gaps in the popular music repertoire. Ray Noble had to settle for third choice but compensated for it by writing imaginative and exciting scores which were to set a high standard for dance-band arrangements for many years to come. He minimized his disadvantages still further by writing his own hit songs: 'Goodnight Sweetheart' in 1931, 'Love Is The Sweetest Thing' and 'By The Fireside' in 1932, and 'The Very Thought Of You' in 1934.

Choosing the musicians for his sessions was the first step in his constant quest for perfection. While he was at HMV there were some he engaged whenever they were available to him: Max Goldberg, his lead trumpet, and Lew Davis, trombonist, both with Ambrose. George Smith and Bob Wise on saxophones; Eric Siday, Reg Pursglove and Jean Pougnet on violins, all from the Savoy. Norman Payne, trumpet, lately with the Fred Elizalde band; Bill Harty, his friend and later his manager, soon to be the drummer with Roy Fox and Lew Stone. Others were Tony

Thorpe and Ted Heath, trombones, Nat Gonella, trumpet, Harry Jacobson, piano, Albert Harris, guitar, Ernest Ritte and Reg Pink, saxophones—each one holding down a top job in the West End.

At first, Noble tried a number of singers: Sam Browne and Elsie Carlisle from Ambrose's band; Jack Plant, first with Pete Mandell's Orchestra and later with Roy Fox; Pat O'Malley, with Ray Starita and Jack Hylton; and Val Rosing, the singer with Henry Hall's BBC Dance Orchestra. Then one day, Bill Harty turned up for a session, bringing Al Bowlly with him. Noble recalls the occasion: 'I think Al hadn't been in London very long, and Bill Harty brought him along and said we should give him a try. I asked Al if he sang printed keys, and he said, yes. I didn't realize at the time that he was so anxious to work that if I'd said, would you climb trees by your tail? he'd have said yes too! Consequently, the first few records he made with me were a third too high. Actually his voice was not printed key at all—it's a bit lower than that.'

Whatever those initial difficulties, there can be no doubt that once Ray Noble had heard Al Bowlly, he was certain that he had found the ideal singer for his band. 'I got along very well with Al', he says. 'He trusted my judgement. When I found his vocal range I picked songs more carefully for him. I rehearsed routines with him, and when unconsciously he drifted into doing things that I didn't think were good, I steered him off. I'd say, "Al, you're singing almost three-quarters of a bar behind in this song because you're trying to sell the pathos of it. You can do it and still keep a little bit more on the beat. And it will sound better."'

Al listened, and learned. From November 1930, when he made his first record with The New Mayfair Orchestra, until December 1937, when they said goodbye in New York and went their separate ways, Ray Noble rarely used another singer. In the fickle world of dance music, it was a most remarkable relationship.

In the early months of 1931, while waiting to take his place with the new Roy Fox band at The Monseigneur, Al's recordings with Ray Noble were steadily enhancing his reputation. In January, he was heard with a small jazz combination which included Norman Payne on trumpet, Payne's brother Laurie on alto and baritone saxes, Harry Hines on clarinet, Jock Fleming on trombone, Bill Harty on drums and Spike Hughes on bass. The song was 'Allah's Holiday' and, reviewing the record, *Melody Maker* praised 'that much improved and now supreme British dance singer, Al Bowlly'. In February, HMV released two titles by The New Mayfair Orchestra: 'How Could I Be Lonely' and 'I'm Telling The World She's Mine'. *Melody Maker* again noted Al's contribution: ' . . . Al Bowlly, who demonstrates here that without any shadow of doubt he is the leading style singer in the country. His phrasing, diction and intonation are superb, whilst the individualism he manages to get into his renderings is really amazing.'

Between 1930 and 1932, Ray Noble recorded more than two hundred titles with vocals by Al Bowlly. So successful were they that by 1932 HMV had been persuaded to break its rule concerning the anonymity of its Light Music Director and label the records, 'Ray Noble and The New Mayfair Orchestra' and, the following year, simply 'Ray Noble And His Orchestra'.

When Ray Noble first met Al Bowlly, he found him flat broke and desperate. But by May of the following year his illustrious career, first with Roy Fox and then with Lew Stone, had begun. From then on, Noble was forced to share his singer's time and his growing fame. The logistics of a Ray Noble session were always complex; somehow he had to find a morning or an afternoon when as many as possible of his favourite musicians (all of them with full date books) were free to work for him. It is the measure of Al Bowlly's importance to him that those recording dates were invariably arranged around his availability. He rarely missed a Ray Noble recording session.

White Tie and Tails

'In those days they used to say that the doorman was the man you had to get by. It was his job to keep the undesirables out, and if he was a good doorman, he would probably know the names of ninety per cent of the clientele. If he thought somebody wasn't suitable to go downstairs or was drunk, or for some reason undesirable, he would simply say "Have you booked?" And if they said "No", he would say "I'm sorry, the restaurant is full." '

In the summer of 1931, another name was added to the list of select hotels and supper clubs where the best dance music could be heard: a list headed by the Mayfair (Ambrose), the Café Anglais (Harry Roy), the Dorchester (Jack Jackson), the San Marco (Maurice Winnick) and the Savoy (Carroll Gibbons). Now *the* doorman to know in the West End was the man at The Monseigneur restaurant, where Roy Fox's new band was playing.

The restaurant was located in the basement of 215 Piccadilly (now a cinema), on the corner between Piccadilly and Lower Regent Street. Jack Upson, managing director of the Dolcis shoe company, had acquired the corner building; as the basement was empty, he decided to turn it into a restaurant, in which he might entertain his lady friends. As money was no object to him at that time, he spared no expense in creating the appropriate ambience. Joyce Stone (who later became the wife of Roy Fox's pianist Lew Stone) attended the opening night, on 27 May:

> I hadn't been invited—the opening night was by invitation only—but I happened to be at a twenty-first birthday party at the Trocadero, given by Jack Upson's nephew. And at the end of the party, he said 'Let's go to The Monseigneur—it's Uncle Jack's opening night.' So the four of us trooped along in evening dress, and to our amazement got past the doorman,

went downstairs and danced for about ten minutes. Then the band stopped for a short interval and, as all the tables were full, we had nowhere to sit, so we gracefully had to come out again! But it was great fun—it was really something quite extraordinary. Very exciting to somebody like myself, who was very young at the time.

After that, Joyce Stone became a regular patron:

> It was the most beautiful restaurant. It was all gilt, the walls were maroon silk. You descended a very elaborate staircase with a very lush carpet. The first door was the ladies' cloakroom; then there was a small door which I later discovered went round the back to the band's rostrum; then you went down again and there was a gentlemen's cloakroom, and that was very impressive because the cloakroom attendant was dressed as a Monseigneur! He had a white wig and a blue velvet coat with lace ruffles. The head waiter who showed you to your table was also dressed in the same kind of uniform. The bar served a special Monseigneur cocktail, which was pale blue. I imagine its base was gin. I had two sips and saw everything in triplicate so I gave up drinking it! There was a gallery running round two sides of the restaurant where you could go if you weren't dressed: a lot of undergraduates used to go there late at night. For ten and sixpence they could have bacon and eggs and coffee.

In the main restaurant, you rarely saw a black tie. White tie and tails was the order of the day. And nobody cut a finer figure in a tailcoat than the leader of the band, Roy Fox. He claims:

> Even to this day people talk more about my tails than they do about my music! I remember once that King Alphonso of Portugal came up to the stand to ask me where I'd had my tails made. I thought it was rather a curious thing for a king to ask a bandleader! In fact, I told him that I owed my tails, and the way I wore them, to Jack Buchanan, who was a great pal of mine. I'd met him in Hollywood when he was doing a film out there. And when I arrived in London, Jack came to my opening night at the Café de Paris. I was wearing a tuxedo

then, with a terrific bow tie I'd bought in New York—very long, sort of shoestring tie with a white stripe running through it. I went over to Jack's table in our first break, and he said 'Roy, do you mind if I make one suggestion?' And I said 'Sure, what's that?' I thought he was going to tell me something about the band, or the way we were playing. He said 'You see everybody's wearing tails and white ties?' and I said 'Yeah, I noticed that.' And he said 'Well, that's what they wear over here. In the States they wear tuxedos, but not here. I wish you'd let me take you to my tailor tomorrow.' Which he did, and that's how I started wearing tails.

In the early days of The Monseigneur, Roy Fox was the star name. Billed as 'Roy Fox, the Whispering Cornetist', he played the quietest trumpet in the West End. On record, tightly muted, it sounds more like a violin than a trumpet. His signature tune was 'Whispering'. 'In those days,' Roy Fox recalls, 'the bandleaders were comparable to film stars. They were *the* attraction of any club: and you could see the way the eyes of the girls as they were dancing past would automatically be drawn to the bandleader. But I soon noticed that Al Bowlly was beginning to attract one or two glances. In fact, if it was a choice between the bandleader or the vocalist, I think on most occasions Al won out! Because he was a good-looking guy—he had a marvellous smile, and good teeth, and a very good appearance. I don't think he had any difficulty with the ladies.'

'You couldn't help it,' remembers Joyce Stone. 'If you were dancing past him, you instinctively looked at Al. His Adam's apple used to fascinate me. It wobbled! He had an enormous amount of charm, very, very attractive eyes, and a lovely smile.' From his chair in the brass section, trumpet-player Nat Gonella used to count the admiring glances directed towards the bandstand: 'You could see their eyes looking over or under their partner's shoulder, or round the back. And all looking at Al Bowlly, of course! Although I used to get one or two glances myself—especially when the Prince of Wales was on the floor. He used to give me a wink over the shoulder of the lovely lady he was dancing with. Because people thought he and I looked very much alike in those days. He was a great fan, the Prince of Wales. But he never paid to get in!'

Under royal patronage, The Monseigneur soon became the 'in' place for the 'in' crowd—members of London's high society, and showbiz celebrities. One evening the guest list included the Prince of Wales, Hoagy Carmichael, Noël Coward, Lady Diana Cooper, and the Maharanee of Sarawak with her two beautiful daughters. But any fraternization between the band and the patrons was out of the question. Only the bandleader could join customers at their table. The musicians were 'staff': 'If they'd had a kitchen entrance at The Monseigneur,' says Nat Gonella, 'then we'd certainly have had to use it!' Unlike the Grand Hotel, Calcutta, where Al and his fellow-musicians had taken their meals alongside the planters and their wives, supper was served for The Monseigneur band in the top floor of the building. A trestle table was set up in the middle of this huge empty floor-space, illuminated by one hanging, unshaded lightbulb, and here the band was served their simple evening meal. Afterwards, while Mantovani and his Typica Orchestra filled in on the bandstand downstairs, Al Bowlly and his pals played solo or poker—at which he excelled. Occasionally the card game would develop into horseplay: 'We'd gag and things like that,' says Nat, 'and sometimes one of us would have a go at someone, and the other guy would grab you—and before you knew where you were, you were on the floor trying to wrestle. Al would get me pinned down in two seconds flat and I couldn't move. Very tough guy, he was.' After their break, they were back on the stand for another stint of continuous 'music for dancing' until 3 am, with Al doing the vocals on 'Sweet and Lovely', *'Cheri, C'est Vous'*, and 'Without a Song' (the Prince of Wales's favourite).

In September 1931, Roy Fox was invited to go along to the BBC to meet Mr Gerald Cock: 'He was in charge of the outside broadcasts of dance music at that time. He called me into his office, and said that he'd heard I had a nice band, and asked me if I'd like to broadcast. I said, "Yes, I'd love to," so he arranged an audition, we got the job and started to broadcast every Wednesday night at 10.30.'

A contract for a weekly, late-night, live broadcast was, in the early 'thirties, the prize most eagerly contested by the rival bandleaders. Between 1929 and 1933, the number of radio licences doubled. All over the country, people were tuning in to the vicarious enjoyment of a night out in the West End, and becoming hooked on the elegant, sophisticated music of the dance bands. The first broadcast by Roy Fox and his Monseigneur band was quite an event, and up in Bridlington, Yorkshire, a young string bass player called Tiny Winters didn't want to miss it:

> I'd just become a professional musician, and had joined a six-piece band accompanying a little concert party in the Pavilion. We were a strange mixture of musicians—I was really the only jazz-minded one among them. I had a radio, which I'd rigged up at the digs. It was one with a spring copper aerial, which I'd had to fix to the gas tap, and I used to sit there late at night, with my headphones on, copying down as much of the music as I could. Once I fell asleep, and woke up to find myself nearly strangled by the headphone cable! Anyway, I'd read in the *Melody Maker* that this new Roy Fox band was going to broadcast from The Monseigneur, so that night I tore home after the show, tuned in, heard the band and thought it was just great. I mean, I came from Hackney, from a nice home, but a poor one: but when you listened in to the radio and heard these sounds coming from the Savoy, or the Dorchester, or The Monseigneur, it was really like tuning into a dream world. Little did I think, as I listened to the Roy Fox band that night, that in nine months' time I would be playing with them.

For their first broadcast from The Monseigneur, the band made no special concessions, except to blow a little bit louder than 'Whispering' Roy Fox would normally allow. A card was displayed at the side of the band, saying 'BAND NOW BROADCASTING'. This was still a novelty. Occasionally customers would have to be restrained from attempting to broadcast their own messages over the microphone, but in general, says Roy Fox, it was 'like a big party all the time'.

The effect of the broadcasts was staggering. A mass of fan-mail followed the first transmissions, taking the band completely by surprise. They had had no conception of the size of the radio audience, and were not at all prepared for the kind of adulation they were now receiving. The centre of attention was Al Bowlly.

By 1931 it is obvious that the crooners were beginning to emerge from the bands. Before radio, they had been relegated to a place in the ranks alongside the musicians, from which they would step forward for their 32-bar 'vocal refrains', after which they returned to the relative anonymity of the rhythm section. But the radio listeners wanted to know the man behind the voice: anonymity was challenged, and the crooner became a personality. Al Bowlly was quite unprepared for this. Being entirely without vanity or pretension, he had no sense of himself as a celebrity, and had no ambition to be anything other than a musician among musicians. He certainly enjoyed the extra work which the band's increasing popularity brought in its wake. The recording sessions with Decca were stepped up from monthly to fortnightly, and then weekly. Next Roy Fox was invited to put his band on stage, in 'ciné-variety' shows at Paramount cinemas throughout London. On stage, the band was expected to put on a show, and Roy Fox took as his model the elaborately produced extravaganzas with which Jack Hylton had made his name all over Europe: a combination of comedy, acrobatics, dance routines and spectacular stage effects, on a solid basis of jazz and dance music. 'Keep it moving' was the rule, as Roy Fox discovered. 'You could hardly go on stage and just sit down and play your music: you had to keep the audience entertained. So, if it was a cowboy tune, we'd have a covered wagon on the stage, and a fire, and cowboys sitting round it singing "Wagon Wheels". There was another tune called "Minnie the Moocher's Wedding Day", for which we'd dress up the members of the band as the different characters in the song, and they would act it out in a visual way. In fact, they used to say that there was more entertainment within my band-show than on the rest of the bill put together!'

Occasionally the band would 'double' theatres, playing two different spots in one night—for instance, Stratford East and Holborn Empire—before making a frantic dash back to The Monseigneur to start work just before midnight. There was new material to learn each week, and rarely enough time for adequate rehearsal. Joyce Stone recalls an evening in The Monseigneur when she noticed that Al was singing with his hands held out in a strange position—arms outstretched, palms towards him. 'I wondered why. Then, as I was dancing past—and he knew me by this time, by my first name—he very quickly turned one hand towards me. And I saw that, in the palm of his hand, he had a piece of paper with minuscule words written on it. It was a new song and he didn't know the lyrics, so this was just a reminder. In those days they had one rehearsal a week which everybody enjoyed, but there was never enough time to prepare the material for a ninety-minute broadcast. So a lot of the new numbers were rehearsed during the week, in the restaurant. I don't suppose the clientele noticed!'

The Roy Fox band was, by all accounts, a very 'matey' band. Indeed, to this day, the surviving members of the band are still in contact with one another, and remain good friends. But Al Bowlly had no special buddies within the group. For all his charming ways—'he would always greet you as if you were the one person in the world he wanted to see'—he kept a part of himself to himself. On the surface, he appears to have been living a quiet life away from work. He had a small flat in Cranbourne Mansions at 26 Charing Cross Road. One bedroom, a sitting-room, tiny kitchen and bathroom, on the top floor. Green carpet, green curtains. The window looked out on to an enclosed well, and on the wall opposite—nobody knows how he did it— Al had stuck a number of travel posters with views of the Mediterranean! This was the only remarkable feature of a flat which, visitors felt, never really looked 'lived in'. Al was used to travelling light. He had no desire to own property, or accumulate personal possessions which might tie him down. And he was often broke. His generous nature earned him the reputation of being a 'soft touch'; it's even said that the down-and-outs would gather round his door every evening in the hopes of catching him for a handout when he left for work. He also enjoyed a bet on the horses and had a number of contacts with Soho bookies' runners. He didn't play golf or football with the other musicians, but 'preferred the indoor sports', says Nat Gonella. He kept himself very fit, with regular visits to the YMCA gym and swimming-pool in Jermyn Street. He rarely drank, but smoked a lot.

His life revolved around his work. If he was singing, he was happy, and for the first six months of The Monseigneur engagement Al sang 'Where Am I? Am I in Heaven?' with genuine feeling. Then, in November 1931, Roy Fox became ill. 'I used to have this pleurisy all the time. I had had it in Hollywood, and sometimes I had to lay up for a month because it's difficult to play the trumpet and have pleurisy at the same time. Because you can't breathe. So I had to go to Switzerland, to sit on top of a mountain for five months.' Before he left, Roy Fox asked Lew Stone to run the band in his absence. Having master-minded the birth of The Monseigneur Band, and written most of the arrangements in its library, Lew Stone was the obvious choice to take over; and he was extremely popular with both musicians and management. He was, however, very reluctant to step into the breach. A modest, self-effacing man, he had no desire to push himself forward into the limelight. He was happy where he was, playing the piano and arranging the band's music. However, on the understanding that it was only a temporary, holding operation, he agreed to take on the band's leadership. Everyone was delighted, and the only anxiety was for Lew's safety on the bandstand. He was a notoriously and spectacularly clumsy man: during a live broadcast he had once sent a whole row of music stands toppling like dominoes, thereby severely taxing the musicians' ability to play from memory. Now, as he assumed the bandleader's position on the edge of the rostrum, his fellow-musicians knew that it was only a matter of time before he took one pace backwards, and fell flat on his back, in white tie and tails, on the dance-floor of The Monseigneur. They were right. He did.

Joyce Stone had her twenty-first birthday party at The Monseigneur.

The management were very kind to young people. If it was your birthday, they always gave you a bunch of carnations and a huge birthday cake, which you had to cut on the premises, while the band played 'Happy Birthday to You', or 'Twenty-

One Today'. Of course you didn't really want to eat it because you'd just had an enormous dinner. But you did sail out of The Monseigneur carrying your carnations. That was rather nice. And I remember that Lew asked me if there was a particular song which I'd like Al to sing. And I said 'Yes', and because 'We're Having a Heatwave' was very popular then, I asked Lew if Al would sing that for me. And he did, and it was a wonderful moment for me.

In the cold light of day, Joyce Stone was often conscious of the gulf that separated the glamorous world of The Monseigneur from the realities of everyday living in London during the Depression. 'I worked in a Working Men's College, where I used to play to the unemployed on a Friday afternoon. The men who came to listen didn't have shoes. Quite often they might have uppers, but the lower part was just cardboard tied on. They were given tea and biscuits, and they were a pretty desperate lot. And the West End was for the wealthy; the people living in the suburbs couldn't afford the bus fare to get there.'

Christmas 1931 saw the unemployment figures climb to a record 2·7 million. A cartoon in *Punch* showed a posh customer inquiring of a shopkeeper, 'Have you noticed any signs yet that people are economizing?'

'Oh, yes, Madam. Even the people who never paid don't buy anything now.'

The *News of the World* was advertising a new portable gramophone for £3·15—'As a Christmas gift—or for the Party—the very thing! A suggestion: Fill the Album in the lid with eight acceptable records and so, for an extra £1, make the gift complete...' Perhaps as a sign of the times, Al Bowlly chose for his Christmas release on HMV a new song by Noël Coward, 'Twentieth Century Blues'. The lyrics express a sentiment far removed from the sugary romanticism that was the staple diet of the dance bands. In fact, it's the nearest approximation to a protest song that the 'thirties produced:

> In this strange illusion, chaos and confusion,
> People seem to lose their way.
> What is there to strive for,

Love or keep alive for?
Say hey! hey!
Call it a day!
Blues,
Nothing to win or lose,
It's getting me down.
Who's escaped those dreary
Twentieth Century Blues?

The Hostess with the Mostest

On 18 December 1931, at the Henrietta Street Register Office, Al Bowlly was married. His bride, Freda Roberts, was a London nightclub hostess. As far as anybody knows she was Al's first wife. She was twenty-one.

It was Nat Gonella who had been responsible for their meeting. Like most of the West End musicians whose passion was jazz, Nat's relaxation, when his work was over at 2 am, was to take himself off to his favourite nightclub, The Bag O'Nails. There he would sit in with the band for a couple of hours and blow out of his system the jazz that an evening of polite Monseigneur dance music had kept so tightly bottled up. After an invigorating jam session, the next stop was Lyons Corner House in Coventry Street for a breakfast of kippers or bacon and egg, and a good gossip with the other jazzers, night owls, insomniacs and inveterate stop-outs who gathered at that friendly meeting place.

On one occasion, Nat ran into Al Bowlly, probably newly surfaced from a poker game somewhere; Al, the eternal bachelor and restless prowler of the night-time streets, was always reluctant to go home to bed. They sat together and ordered coffee. Freda Roberts came in, and Al immediately demanded to know who she was.

'I knew her very well,' says Nat, 'because I used to see her every night at the club. I said, "That's Freda Roberts." He said, "I'd like to meet her." I said, "Well there's no danger there, I'll introduce you to her." I went over to her table, and her eyes were blazing. She said, "Who's that guy with you?" I said, "That's Al Bowlly. Do you want to meet him?" She said yes. So they got together and that was it. Electric. Within a week they were married. And I thought to myself, poor old Al. What have I done?'

Nat Gonella was not the only one to harbour misgivings. When Al announced his marriage to the Lew Stone band, they were flabbergasted. Here was the country's favourite singer, a celebrity who could have made his choice among a thousand women, and he was about to marry a nightclub hostess. 'She was a lovely bird,' says Nat, 'but she had a reputation.'

Freda Roberts had been born in Yorkshire, the daughter of a merchant seaman. When she was seventeen, she met a small-time actor and left home. After a few minor parts in repertory, she left the actor, took a train to London and landed herself a job as a dance hostess at Romano's in the Strand. For this slim, dark-eyed beauty, the pickings were easy and lush. Men thought her fascinating and she found she could earn sixty or seventy pounds in a week. Soon she had progressed from the more or less law-abiding jollifications at Romano's to the headier excitements of the illicit nightclubs around Piccadilly and Soho. At the Bag O'Nails, the drinking and the dancing went on until 5 am and there were parties when the club had closed which continued until long after dawn.

The Bag O'Nails, in a basement in Kingly Street off Regent Street, was run by the legendary Kate Meyrick. Mrs Meyrick, known as 'Ma' to her friends and loyal patrons, was an indomitable Irish lady who, deserted by her husband, a doctor, in 1919, had found herself alone, broke, and with six growing children to support—three boys at Harrow, and three girls at Roedean. A man named Murray Dalton introduced her to London's night life, and in 1921 she opened her first club, The Cecil, which was later to become the notorious '43' Club, so named for its address in Gerrard Street. The '43' was another nightclub which would later impinge upon Al Bowlly's life.

Soon Kate Meyrick had become the undisputed 'Queen of Clubs', and was at one time proprietress of no less than four such establishments. Among them were The Slip-In, The Manhattan, and, grandest of them all, The Silver Slipper in Regent Street, which boasted a glass dance floor.

In her book *The Long Party*, Stella Margetson describes this remarkable woman:

She was completely without glamour and dowdily dressed, with an old velvet cape or a tatty piece of fur draped around her shoulders: a dark, spidery little woman with sharp eyes and a sharp face, belied by the warmth and vitality of her smile when she welcomed her 'boys', as she called her clients, into her web. The list of her members at the '43' read like the pages of *Debrett*, interspersed with a mixture of Bohemian artists and writers, boxers, jockeys and *nouveaux riches*, like the Lancashire millionaire, Jimmie White, who brought six Daimlers full of show-girls one night to a champagne party costing £400.

At a time when nightclubs were quite simply illegal (they sold drink after hours and they had no dancing licence), and when Sir William Joynson-Hicks ('Jix'), the Home Secretary of the day and a resolute kill-joy, was closing them down with vigour and enthusiasm, Mrs Meyrick's clubs were seldom raided, or if they were, there had been sufficient warning of the approach of the Vice Squad for appropriate measures to be taken. Leslie Jackson, a saxophone player who worked at the '43', remembers one of these occasions: 'Kathy [one of Kate's daughters], was upstairs taking the half-crown entrance fees. After a phone call came through, she rushed down to give a message. Then we all traipsed through the scenery, through a hidden door to number forty-one. When the cops arrived, "43" was clean.'

Kate didn't always escape prosecution. In 1924 she went to Holloway, and again in 1929, when she was sentenced to eighteen months for her involvement in the Sergeant Goddard drama, a bribery and corruption case which shook the Metropolitan Police to its foundations. When she was released her adoring patrons threw a party for her, at which they sang:

Come all you birds
And sing a roundelay,
Now Mrs Meyrick's
Out of Holloway.

Stella Margetson concludes the Kate Meyrick story: 'Twice more she went to gaol, but in 1932, again in front of the bench, she gave "an honourable undertaking to have no more to do with nightclubs"—and a year later she was dead, though not before she had married three of her daughters into the peerage: Ethel to the racing motorist Lord Kinnoull, Dorothy to Lord de Clifford and Kathy to the Earl of Craven.'

Nightclubs like the '43' and The Bag O'Nails would employ six or more dance hostesses, whose duties were to sit, when invited to do so, with unaccompanied male guests, dance with them, make lively conversation and coax them into buying the best (and the most expensive) that the house had to offer: champagne rather than Scotch or gin, Havana cigars rather than cigarettes, and enormous boxes of chocolates. As the evening wore on and the customers became increasingly drunk, these predatory ladies of the night could invent a dozen ways of persuading their befuddled escorts to part with their money. A selection of soft toys was always on sale—giant pandas and huge teddy bears, monstrous playthings which, it seemed, were available nowhere else but in nightclubs, and which, once purchased, were invariably returned to the management to be 'sold' several more times. Leslie Jackson remembers: 'I have seen, among other devilries, a stoned customer presented with the bill three or four times, and him paying it each time.' Hostesses were never paid by the club. They earned only what their customers were willing to pay them for their geisha-like services. Such arrangements as they might make after leaving the premises were, the management allowed, entirely their own affair.

It isn't surprising that the dance-band musicians felt an affinity with the nightclub hostesses. They both inhabited the same carefree nocturnal world; the girls were pretty and available, generous and undemanding. Many a musician could count the happy hours spent in their company. It was an easy-come, easy-go relationship. When Al Bowlly married Freda Roberts, he was quite unable to understand the appalled reaction of his colleagues. With his conventional *petit bourgeois* Christian upbringing, he would have made a clear distinction between the casual affairs which were the end products of his nightly prowlings and a romantic encounter which had stirred his deepest feelings. He was in love with a lively attractive girl and she was in love with him. The most natural thing in the world was that they should marry.

1 Jimmy Lequime's band in Calcutta (*l to r*) Claude Maguire, Monia Liter, Jacker Lippe (behind), Jimmy Lequime, Al Bowlly, Eddie Beecher, Joe Speelman

Al Bowlly at home around 1930

3 With the Roy Fox band at The Monseigneur

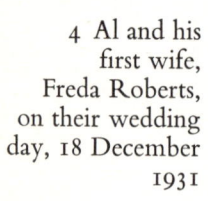

4 Al and his first wife, Freda Roberts, on their wedding day, 18 December 1931

5 Roy Fox and The Monseigneur Band: (*l to r*) Harry Berly, Billy Amstell, Ernest Ritte, Bill Harty (behind), Roy Fox, Al Bowlly, Don Stutely, Lew Stone, Joe Ferrie, Nat Gonella, Sid Buckman

6 Lew Stone and The Monseigneur Band: (*l to r*) Harry Berly, Ernest Ritte, Bill Harty, Joe Crossman, Jim Easton, Tiny Winters, Al Bowlly, Lew Stone, Lew Davis, Eddie Carroll, Nat Gonella, Joe Ferrie, Alfie Noakes

7 Lew Stone's Monseigneur Band in 1932 (Sallon)

8 Lew Stone and The Monseigneur Band: (*l to r*) Harry Berly, Ernest Ritte, Joe Crossman, Jim Easton, Al Bowlly, Bill Harty, Lew Davis, Eddie Carroll, Nat Gonella, Tiny Winters, Joe Ferrie, Alfie Noakes

9 Ray Noble and the band in Holland: (*l to r*) Harry Berly, Freddy Gardner, Bill Harty, Tiny Winters, (unknown), Nat Gonella, Ray Noble, Al Bowlly, Cecil Norman, Bob Wise, Alfie Noakes

10 Ray Noble's band at a recording session

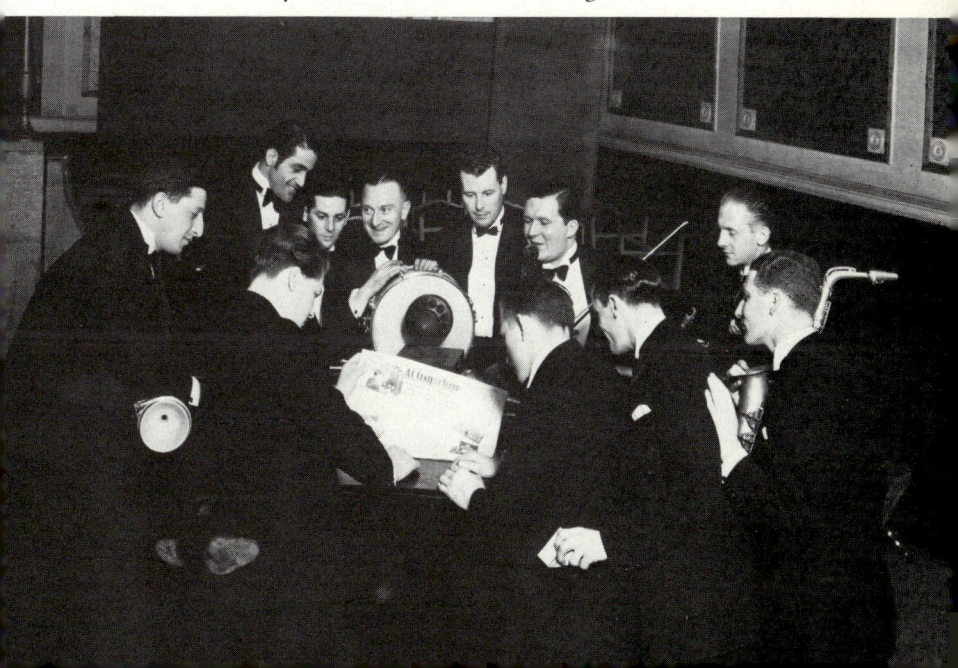

11 Ray Noble's recording band at the HMV studios: (*l to r*) Max Goldberg, Harry Smith, Tony Thorpe, Bill Shakespeare, Norman Payne, Dave Thomas, Harry Jacobson, Bill Evetts, Bill Harty (in front), Al Bowlly, Ray Noble, Reg Pursglove, Bob Wise, Eric Siday, Ernest Ritte, Jean Pougnet

12 In the Rainbow Room, New York City. Al and Ray Noble have joined Anna Neagle and Herbert Wilcox at their table

13 Ray Noble and the Rainbow Room orchestra. Al is at the mike and the trombonist on the far left is Glenn Miller

14 Making an early commercial

15 Al with Sidney Lipton at Grosvenor House

16 Al at the BBC with Pat Hyde and Stanley Barnett (seated)

The idea that they might perhaps live together for a while would simply never have occurred to him.

What most upset his friends and colleagues was that he should so lightly throw away his chances. Every night of the week at The Monseigneur, debutantes and the daughters of the rich lingered longingly in front of the bandstand, flirting with him, vying with one another for the favour of one of his special smiles —any one of them, the boys in the band reckoned, could have been his for the asking. Nat Gonella affirms: 'There was the Maharanee of Sarawak. She had two lovely daughters and they were Princesses. Princesses, no more, no less. They used to give the eye to Al, and one of them eventually married Harry Roy [the other married an all-in wrestler]. I really thought that Al was going to marry one of those.'

Al's marriage to Freda lasted just three weeks. Some say he returned to their flat one night after work to find her with another man. Whatever the reason, they parted. Two years later, in January 1934, Freda got her final decree—Al having done the gentlemanly thing and provided her with grounds for divorce—adultery.

Al saw little of Freda during those two years; wounded and unhappy, he made sure that their paths never crossed. Freda was less considerate of her ex-husband's feelings; when Lew Stone's band moved from The Monseigneur to the Café Anglais in November 1933, she took to frequenting the place with one or another of her constantly changing escorts. The Anglais, in Leicester Square, was somewhat lower on the social scale than The Monseigneur. Nat Gonella recalls one of the encounters between the estranged couple: 'I'd be watching Al's face and it would just go white, sort of drained of blood. I'd wonder what was happening because he looked just like Dracula. And I'd look, and there was Freda Roberts dancing round the floor with a very nice gentleman.' The story goes that her presence in the restaurant upset him so much that, in desperation, he put his problem to some of his underworld friends, who obliged by paying her a visit and persuading her, none too gently, never to do it again.

The gangsters of London during the 'twenties and 'thirties were mostly associated with the Turf. They extorted protection money from the course bookmakers and in return they defended favoured pitches against competitors and collected betting debts from recalcitrant punters. The racetracks of Windsor, Epsom Downs and, in particular, the Brighton track at Lewes, were the scenes of many a pitched battle between rival gangs, and, in 1922, Augustus and Enrico Cortesi were found guilty of the attempted murder of Charles and Harry Sabini. Graham Greene was to enshrine the gangsters and their world in his novel of 1938, *Brighton Rock*.

The Sabini brothers, sons of an Italian father and an English mother, were the leaders of the most feared of the gangs. In 1928, Charles Sabini and a man named George Wood were charged with committing a vicious assault at Brighton racetrack upon three men; the witnesses suffered a simultaneous lapse of memory and declared that it was a case of mistaken identity. Sabini was discharged; his henchman was fined £8. In 1936, there was a celebrated confrontation at Lewes. The Sabinis, greatly outnumbered, found themselves up against thirty members of the Hoxton gang. In the battle which followed, razors, iron bars, coshes and knuckledusters were used, and sixteen of the Hoxton gang went to prison for a total of fifty-three and a half years.

The gangsters were denizens of the same night-time world that some musicians inhabited during their off-duty hours. They would meet around the 'speilers', the illicit basement gambling clubs which proliferated around Soho in those days. For their part, the gangsters enjoyed their acquaintanceship with musicians and actors, and would boast about their friends, the stars. Al Bowlly's particular friend was Harry Sabini, and it was doubtless Harry and one or two of his heavies who used their powers of persuasion on Freda Roberts.

Freda told her own sad story to two *Daily Express* reporters. First she spoke of her marriage to Al and of the life she continued to lead when it was all over: 'There was a week-end flat in Paris, a mink coat to add to the jewellery. And all the time the parties got gayer. I remember one I went to in Upper Berkeley Street in 1935. Everyone was sprawled on the floor, deliriously happy. They all yelled: "Give Freda some." "Some" was a shot of heroin.' Soon she was hopelessly hooked. In 1938 she was fined ten pounds for possessing drugs at her flat in Phoenix House, Charing Cross Road. But she could not kick the habit. 'I had six months in a mental hospital on the order of a London magistrate. It was a nightmare. When I came out, my hair was white. I had to wear a black stole over my evening gowns to hide the needle marks on my left arm.'

All her assets soon disappeared in support of her addiction—her bank balance, her mink, her jewels. She found a convent where the sisters cured her and taught her to cook. But she found that she had only replaced one addiction with another: 'Only gin for breakfast could take the shake out of my hands.' The *Express* reporters had traced her to a Leeds boarding house: 'She has £39 in the bank: a few clothes. On New Year's Eve she will go back to the convent which cured her. There she plans to spend the rest of her life as a two-pound, ten-shillings a week cook.' That was in 1951. Nothing more has been heard of Freda Roberts, the girl the boys in the band used to call the hostess with the mostest.

Top of the Bill

On April Fool's Day 1932, Roy Fox resumed his place in front of The Monseigneur Band. The well-cut tails didn't fit quite so well, as he was now two stone heavier than at the time of his collapse five months earlier. He was also considerably richer. The Monseigneur management had kept him on full salary during his Swiss convalescence, and the band had continued to play as 'Roy Fox and his Band'. Under Lew Stone's direction, they had gone from strength to strength. *Melody Maker* reported:

> Lew Stone has performed miracles, and has brought the band to such a pitch of perfection that its name is on the tip of everybody's tongue. The organization has achieved the almost unprecedented triumph of being both stylish enough for the fans, and at the same time amusing enough for the most ingenuous of the masses. The band has not only achieved an almost unrivalled reputation on the air and in the ballroom, but its records have reached a pitch of perfection which is nothing short of remarkable, while recently it has fulfilled engagements in the talkie studios of Elstree, which have been both lucrative and prolific.

In 1931, Lew Stone had been appointed Musical Director for British and Dominion films at Elstree studios. Over the next few years, he was responsible for the music on more than forty films—conducting, arranging, fixing and composing. Wherever possible, he secured a screen appearance for The Monseigneur Band. In *A Night Like This*, an Aldwych Farce Company film released in March 1932, the band appeared in several cabaret scenes, and Al Bowlly sang 'If Anything Happened to You' and 'In London on a Night Like This'. These two titles were also released on a Decca recording but, cryptically, the band on the label is billed as

'The Rhythm Maniacs'. There is no doubt that it *is* The Monseigneur Band, though why Lew Stone chose to use a pseudonym remains a mystery. In every other way, he had been Roy Fox's faithful steward, keeping the band together, expanding its potential, and safeguarding the leader's interests during his Swiss sojourn.

Once reinstated, Roy Fox showed no inclination to tinker with Lew Stone's highly successful policy. He was shrewd enough to know that Stone's ideas, though occasionally eccentric, were the major factor in the band's success. At times Fox appears to have been totally bemused by the very English brand of 'silly-ass' comedy that now flourished in the band. In the Pathé film archive, there's a short newsreel sequence in which the Roy Fox band sings a new comedy foxtrot entitled 'It Ain't No Fault of Mine'. It's very evident that Roy Fox prefers not to join in the chorus, and the expression on his face is one of sheer amazement as Nat Gonella and Joe Ferrie rattle through a succession of excruciating puns: 'If the man who steals your watch gets "time", It ain't no fault of mine!'

Lew Stone exploited the vocal talents of every musician in the band. He later said: 'If I didn't think Al Bowlly was right for a particular song, I would give it to a musician who could interpret it better. Just as everybody played section lead at one time or another, so everybody sang. I did plenty of vocals myself. I was concerned with the emotional output of each person—not whether he'd ever sung before. If they were able to croak in the right way on a certain number, I would get them to sing it. And they were all game for anything.' Did Al Bowlly ever object to the other players muscling in on the vocal department? Absolutely not, says Nat Gonella: 'He didn't have a jealous bone in his body.'

On 1 August 1932, the Roy Fox band opened at the London Palladium. Under the headline 'Roy Fox Hits the High Spots', *Melody Maker* commented on Roy's self-effacing style of leadership: 'Roy himself—more immaculate, debonair and dignified than ever—announced each number through a mike, by means of which the vocal efforts of the boys were also transmitted to the loudspeaker situated above the auditorium. Beyond announcing, and giving his boys the tempo to commence each number, Roy himself did practically nothing. Many contend that he should have taken a more active part in the show. We do not agree, for Roy's example of completely restrained showmanship was extremely effective—far more so than over-zealous windmill antics could ever have been.' Nat Gonella has another explanation for Roy's unobtrusive leadership, which is that he was 'a bit lazy'.

For its two-week stint at the Palladium, the band featured a new bass-player, Tiny Winters. Winters had graduated from his concert party in Bridlington to occasional work with London pick-up bands, and then found himself playing at the wedding of Ambrose's drummer Max Bacon. Ambrose was present at this wedding party, and was so impressed by the young bass-player that he offered him a job. 'But I was too rough for Ambrose,' says Tiny:

> I played 'slap-bass', like the coloured jazz musicians. Ambrose had a much more sedate type of orchestra, very precise, and I didn't fit in. After a couple of weeks Ambrose decided to look for another bass-player, and he chose Don Stutely, who was then playing with Roy Fox. I immediately went and auditioned for the Fox band—and got the job. So it was a straight swap of bass-players!
>
> They were a very nice bunch of fellows in the Roy Fox band. I was a bit green in those days, and they were all very helpful to me. Lew Stone acted like an elder brother towards me, and looked after me. Al Bowlly was always very friendly to me, too, always greeted me with a big smile . . . That's really the way I remember him. Sometimes when I hear tunes come up on the radio—'Goodnight Sweetheart', 'Buddy, Can You Spare a Dime?', 'You're Blasé'—certain numbers take me right back to The Monseigneur. I can almost hear the people, and smell the restaurant . . . It gets so real. And I can see Al standing up there—I think when I started playing there he was still using a megaphone . . . He was a very, very nice guy.
>
> He was very boyish at times, he acted just like a little boy. I remember an occasion when we were engaged for a theatrical garden party in Regents Park. It was a tremendous affair, with

hundreds of people involved. All the shows in the West End used to take a stall. Noël Coward ran it, and the proceeds went to the Actors' Orphanage. After the band had played, Al and I decided to have a go at a coconut shy! After about two tries, I knocked one down and was given it, so I thought 'I'll have another go'. Al had a go, too. It ended up with us going round all the coconut shies, and we wound up with about seventeen coconuts! Al said 'Come back to my place for tea, and we'll share them out.' So we went to his flat, had tea, and then we started. He chose first, and chose the biggest. Then it was my turn, and I took the next biggest, and so on until we'd worked our way down to the smallest! That was Al—he could be very boyish at times.

In September Roy Fox fell out with The Monseigneur management. Encouraged by the success of the Palladium shows, he wanted to extend the band's variety activities, but owner Jack Upson objected, on the grounds that this would take them away from The Monseigneur too often. Fox refused to budge, and on 24 September he was given a month's notice to quit. Upson sent for Lew Stone, and invited him to form a band and take over the duties of musical director. Lew Stone didn't jump at the offer: 'I said I'd need several days to think it over. He said he'd give me as long as it took to walk round the block. I'd got halfway round when I found myself thinking what I might do with a band of my own, so I went straight back and said "Yes".'

At the time, Lew Stone had every intention of forming a completely new band. But The Monseigneur musicians cornered him as soon as they heard the news. 'I told them "You'll have to stay with Fox, you're all under contract to him." They said: "What's that got to do with it? Let him take us to court—we'd love it." So I said: "Well, it's up to you. If you want to stay, I can still fit you in. I haven't got as far as booking new musicians." And that's the reason they came to me. I did *not* take over Fox's band. The band took *me* over.'

Only one musician, trumpeter Sid Buckman, chose to stay with Roy Fox, who was moving to a new base at the Café Anglais. To fill his chair in The Monseigneur Band, Lew Stone contacted

Alfie Noakes, then playing with Sidney Kyte's band at the Piccadilly Hotel. They met, by secret arrangement, in a Piccadilly garage and Noakes agreed to come over to The Monseigneur. Stone's next move was to persuade Jack Upson to pay for two extra musicians—one brass, one sax. He agreed, and Lew Stone then wooed Lew Davis (trombone) away from Jack Hylton and Joe Crossman (alto sax) from Ambrose.

The new band was billed as 'Lew Stone and The Monseigneur Band'. Their debut was scheduled for Monday, 24 October. On Saturday, 22 October, the bombshell dropped. Roy Fox applied for an injunction against Al Bowlly 'to restrain him, during the continuance of his contract with Roy Fox, from playing or performing at any establishment except as directed by Fox.' Sitting in chambers, Mr Justice Lawrence granted the injunction. It was the first and only time in his career that Al Bowlly was prevented by law from singing.

Two days later, the new band was launched at The Monseigneur, but the guitar chair in the centre of the band was empty. *Melody Maker* headlined the 'Colossal Promise of All-British Band', but added that 'the band's opening was somewhat handicapped by the fact that Al Bowlly could not play or sing with it, and the routine of the numbers had to be altered at the last moment.'

What provoked Roy Fox to litigate against Al Bowlly? He appeared to have acknowledged the impossibility of keeping the musicians under contract, against their will. He had given them a free choice: to go with him to the Café Anglais, or stay at The Monseigneur with Lew Stone. Was it then an afterthought, to try and retain the services of Al Bowlly? To this day, Roy Fox refuses to talk about the split, and Lew Stone, interviewed before his death in 1970, was reluctant to open old wounds. He had warned the musicians at the time that there might be a lot of nasty talk. He told them to say nothing: 'The sooner it's forgotten, the better. If you don't answer it, it'll die.'

If nothing else, the incident shows a growing awareness of Al Bowlly's potential. He was a real asset that Roy Fox was very reluctant to lose. In the event, on the day after The Monseigneur opening, an application was made on behalf of Bowlly to Mr

Justice McCardie, who ruled that the contract with Fox related specifically to The Monseigneur Restaurant engagement and could not be binding elsewhere. The injunction was lifted, and Al Bowlly resumed his duties as vocalist to Lew Stone. The whole band breathed a sigh of relief, and that night there was a special celebration in The Monseigneur's attic bandroom.

It was in the late autumn of 1932 that the Lew Stone bandwagon began to gather force. 'I believe', Stone boasted to *Melody Maker*, 'that it is possible to produce a band in this country which in many respects may rival any in the world, even Duke Ellington's or the Dorsey brothers. We may not have available players of such supreme virtuosity as some of the American stars, but we can make up for this with ensemble and arrangements, and I give myself three months only to prove my claims to the world.'

He certainly had the team to do it. He had taken pains to assemble the very best musicians in town, and his full line-up read like a 'Who's Who' of 1930s' instrumental stars: on saxophones, Joe Crossman, Harry Berly, Ernest Ritte and Jim Easton; on trumpets, Nat Gonella and Alfie Noakes; on trombones, Lew Davis and Joe Ferrie; piano, Eddie Carroll; string bass, Tiny Winters; drums, Bill Harty; and guitar and vocals, Al Bowlly.

Lew Stone had also given some thought to the needs of his audience.

> The first question in formulating the band was who did I want to play to? To one set of people who bought a certain type of jazz journal? I started thinking about the different phases that people go through: as youngsters, looking for excitement; in their twenties, falling in love; getting older, gathering more experience. With maturity, they still receive the stimulation of rhythmic pulses, and they don't want to lose that beat. But they need to hear music where their brain is utilized. Then I thought: 'Well, I can't please everybody. But I can please practically all of them most of the time.' And I plumped for putting over programmes which had a pretty wide spectrum. Listening to our Tuesday night radio show, people got used to the fact that if there was something they disliked, it wouldn't last for more than three minutes. Either side of one of our more

outlandish things—say 'Call of the Freaks'—I would have maybe a warm sentimental number sung by Al Bowlly, and Joe Crossman playing a nice clarinet solo. After that, maybe a light, somewhat humorous number. That's the way I was able to play, in West End society places, music that would have been absolutely unheard of otherwise.

He acknowledged that, as an arranger, he had no special style. 'I don't compose. I select my subject, interpret its true meaning, then put the band *into* the subject. So you always hear that basic subject coming through.' He applied this method to the selection of new material, and caused some anxiety in Tin Pan Alley in the process. Joyce Stone recalls that on his weekly visits to the music publishers he would never allow anyone else to play him a new song.

This used to drive the publishers absolutely mad, because Lew would say, 'I don't want to hear your interpretation—I want to play it my way.' And he would sit down and play very quietly. You could hardly recognize what he was playing, but his mind was working on the double, and he was working out his interpretation. And quite often he would turn a waltz into a fox-trot or a tango, or something altogether remote from the composer's own idea of how it should be. They could hear him making queer noises on the piano, and they would get quite worried, but the end results were always good. Because Lew had superimposed his idea on that music. In the end, the publishers learnt not to try to play anything to Lew!

Lew Stone was the best thing that happened to Al Bowlly. His thoughtful, creative musicianship made him the best possible producer, counsellor, and tutor for Al at this critical stage of his career, with one foot already firmly placed on the stairway to the stars. 'Al Bowlly was a natural,' said Lew in later years. 'I worked very closely with him. I coached him at the piano in the way I wanted him to sing a particular number. He was very responsive.'

The commitment to Lew, from every member of the band, was total. Although rehearsals were conducted in a fairly relaxed manner—Lew believed that too much discipline at rehearsal led to an inhibited performance on the stand—nevertheless the musicians went at their work with gusto and enthusiasm. 'Every new tune was an adventure to us,' said Joe Crossman, 'and we exploited it to the hilt, with everybody in the band contributing ideas.' Joyce Stone agrees: 'There was a wonderful atmosphere and enthusiasm. If you overran your time at rehearsal there was no Union official to say "You've got to pay the boys extra." They didn't expect it. They were enjoying themselves.'

Even for morning rehearsals, after a late night at The Monseigneur, the band would all be present and correct, without grumbles. 'Al Bowlly was the most conscientious worker of us all,' says Tiny Winters. 'He always did his work well, no arguments, very punctual.' The story concerning the day on which he *did* arrive late for rehearsal has now become part of the band's official history, and Al was teased unmercifully about it for years afterwards. The official reporters of the saga are Joe Crossman and Tiny Winters.

> We had already started rehearsals, running through a couple of numbers for notes and phrasing, when Al suddenly burst in like a whirlwind, looking very embarrassed and out-of-breath. He ran straight over to the piano, picked up the music, said 'Is this the song, Lew?' He was very confused, very embarrassed. Lew looked at him and said, 'What on earth's the matter with you, and where have you been?' Al said 'I'm so sorry, I've been trying out a friend's car; it broke down on the Great West Road, and I had to mend the gaskets.' There was a momentary silence. Al looked round and saw an incredulous look on all the boys' faces. Then from behind the drums came Bill Harty's peculiar, high-pitched nanny-goat laugh, which was always guaranteed to set the band off. Soon we were all roaring our heads off at the idea of Al Bowlly getting his cylinder head off, and fitting a new gasket out on the Great West Road! I don't think he knew much about cars, or he wouldn't have made a remark like that. But then Al couldn't tell a lie. He wasn't very successful at it anyway.

The band were unanimous, however, in their admiration for Al's skill, and success, with the ladies. It was a custom within the band to invent a nickname out of each player's most characteristic feature, coupled with a communal Joe. Accordingly, Tiny Winters was known as Joe Golf, Ernest Ritte (a dedicated vegetarian) was Joe Carrot, Lew Davis (a dab hand with a screwdriver) was Joe Fixit, and Lew Stone was Joe Clumsy. Al Bowlly was Joe Sex. 'He had a lot of women interested in him,' recalls Joe Crossman. 'You'd get to hear about this one or that one, a girl from the nightclubs or wherever. But then that was the trend in those days. We were all interested in women.'

In January 1933, Monia Liter, Al's companion in Calcutta and Singapore, arrived in London, hoping to renew their friendship and gain an entrée to the dance band 'magic circle'. On his first evening in the West End, he saw that an American dancer from the Ziegfield Follies called Betty Daly was appearing at the Leicester Square Theatre.

> I had played as her accompanist in Hong Kong, so when I got to London I wanted to see her. I went to the stage door and sent my card round. She came down, and was very pleased to see me. 'What are you doing tonight?' she asked me. 'Absolutely nothing—I'm new here—I don't know the place.' She said 'Why don't you come and have dinner with me? We're going to The Monseigneur.' 'That would be marvellous,' I said. 'Have you got a suit of tails, white tie and so on?' I said 'Of course,' and that night I joined her party at The Monseigneur, and sat at the table alongside Victor McLaglen, Jeanette MacDonald and Douglas Fairbanks. And there on the bandstand was my old friend, Al Bowlly! His face lit up when he saw me, and in the intermission he came over to our table. He said, 'It's wonderful to see you again—please come home with me after the show. I want you to meet my girlfriend, Marjie.' So when The Monseigneur closed, I walked home with him to his flat in Charing Cross Road, not far from the Garrick Theatre. But when we went in, Marjie wasn't there. Al was very upset, because it was after three o'clock in the morning. I could see he was getting excited because I remember from Singapore that he had a nervous habit of clicking the bones in his hands when he was getting tense. Anyway, about half an

hour later, a girl arrived who I assumed to be Marjie. I'm afraid she was a little bit intoxicated. Al took her into the bedroom, closed the door, and then I heard the most terrible racket—things being thrown, screaming, banging, crying. I thought 'This is too much for me,' wrote a little note saying, 'I'm very tired. I've had a long journey from Hong Kong, I'm going home to bed. See you tomorrow,' left it on the table and quietly disappeared out of the house.

Marjie, later to become Al's second wife, came from Devon. Taller than Al, blonde and good-looking, she was a sophisticated girl and worked as a dance hostess at the '43' Club. Unlike Al's first wife Freda, Marjie found approval with Al's fellow musicians. Everybody liked her. 'She was a very good sort', says Ray Noble, 'and very understanding. She knew, after all, that anyone who's a singer is bound to attract a certain amount of interest from the opposite sex. It's inevitable. Marjie took it in her stride. Al didn't make it easy for her, but she understood him very well and he always came back to her. And he never hid anything from her, because it wasn't in his nature. He was absolutely a very simple man: everything for him was either white or black. When he loved, he loved, and when he hated, he hated. And if he hated you, then off came the coat and he was ready to go. But with a little tactful handling he was a charming fellow.'

In February 1933, Al Bowlly sang for England in a competition organized by the *News Chronicle* to see whether English dance-band recordings could hold their own against the American invaders. The public was invited to choose between two records—one English, one American. For England, Al Bowlly sang 'What More Can I Ask?' with Lew Stone and his Monseigneur Band. For America, Bing Crosby sang 'Young and Healthy' with Guy Lombardo and his Royal Canadians. The public was invited to guess the sales of each record: the result was 28,000 for Al Bowlly against 20,000 for Bing. Although this doesn't compare with today's Golden Disc statistics, it certainly indicates the fast-growing public interest in the Lew Stone Band—and in Al Bowlly. His name was now beginning to appear on the record labels, in place of the anonymous 'with vocal refrain'. He was in the recording studios almost every week, with either Ray Noble's New Mayfair Orchestra, or Lew Stone's Monseigneur Band. In the first three months of 1933, he recorded forty-six songs, including 'Sitting in the Dark', 'Let me Give my Happiness to You', 'Standing on the Corner' and 'A Letter to my Mother'. This last was one of Al's personal favourites. Based on a traditional Yiddish song, it had been suggested to Lew Stone by trombonist Lew Davis, whose father had found a copy of the original—*'A Brivele der Mame'*—in a little Jewish bookshop in Aldgate. English words were set to it by Joseph Gilbert and Al Nilke, but in the Lew Stone version Al Bowlly would sing the first chorus in Yiddish, and the next in English. Lew Davis's wife taught Al how to pronounce the Yiddish words, but he needed no coaching in how to project the sentiment.

> I stayed from home, where did I roam?
> I miss my mother's affection.
> Her rocking chair, her silver hair
> Is in my fond recollection . . .
>
> I'll write a letter to my mother.
> And tell her just how much I love her.
> She worries so, but I know
> Angels watch above her . . .

'A Brivele der Mame' was a huge popular success, both as a record and as a much-requested, often-repeated broadcast favourite. Lew Stone's girlfriend Joyce had to be enlisted to help sort through the huge postbag that was now arriving every week at the BBC. Alongside requests for favourite songs, she found a regular theme running through these listeners' letters, along the lines of 'Dear Mr Stone, When can we *see* your wonderful band?'. A large and enthusiastic audience was now waiting impatiently for the first 'live' appearance of Lew Stone and The Monseigneur Band. But Lew Stone had to tread carefully here. The Monseigneur management had taken a tough line with Roy Fox over his extra-curricular activities, and Lew Stone had no desire to jeopardize his base at The Monseigneur by taking on too much, too soon. He decided to start in a quiet way, and took the band to

bookings at a reasonable distance from Piccadilly: suburban theatres like the Davis Theatre in Croydon, the Kingston Empire, the Gaumont Palace, Lewisham, and the Streatham Locarno.

It was a good time to go into variety. The music hall was dying and apart from one or two big names—Gracie Fields, George Formby, the Crazy Gang—there was a real shortage of stars who could top a variety bill. Managers looked to the dance bands for salvation, and wherever they played, Lew Stone and his Monseigneur Band were given pride of place—'top of the bill'. Soon the band began to appear in central London; at the Holborn Empire, they played twice nightly, at 6.30 and at 9.00. They were 'retained for a second week by public demand', with fresh numbers and entirely new supporting acts: The Dinkie Denton Trio (songs, music and dance), Morris and Cowley (burlesque vocal comedians), Stella and Partner (gymnasts), and Lily Moore (with a 'flexible voice and a smile'). But the audience had come to see the band, and for those who had been listening to the radio every Tuesday and could identify by ear every member of the band, it was a moment of real magic when the first bars of 'Oh Monah!', the band's signature tune, were heard from behind the closed tabs. When they opened to reveal the band in dinner-jacketed splendour, there was a roar of delight. From 'Oh Monah!', the band would plunge straight into an up-tempo version of 'Goodbye Blues', with a trumpet solo by Nat Gonella. Then Al Bowlly would come forward, to another roar of approval, to sing '*A Brivele der Mame*', and be rewarded with deafening applause. Joe Crossman would don a crinkly black wig and do a blackface minstrel version of 'Lazy Bones', followed by 'Little Nell'. This was greeted enthusiastically by the audience, who knew it as a radio favourite; now they would see the song acted out. Tiny Winters was Little Nell; Jim Easton was her father, a farmer; Nat Gonella played 'the constabule'; and Al Bowlly was the villain. Easton would begin with the opening chorus:

It was a dark and stormy night
When m'Nelly went away . . .
The rooster's died
And the hens won't lay.

There followed a crash of thunder, and a lighting change, and Al would enter:

'Who's that knocking on my door?'
'It's your Little Nell—
Don't you know me anymore?'

Bowlly as villain would reject Nell, spurning his own baby. Nell, distraught, would be saved by 'the constabule'. Evil punished, virtue rewarded. The scene over, the cast would dance off stage, singing 'and tomorrow night, we'll play East Lynne'. The audience loved it, and were usually still talking excitedly when the band blasted into 'Bugle Call Rag', with timpani breaks from Bill Harty. A new Ray Noble song came next: 'Goodnight Sweetheart', after which Tiny Winters sang 'Oh You Nasty Man' in a very high-pitched voice. (He once got a fan-letter from Paris addressed to *Mademoiselle* Tiny Winters!) After two old favourites, 'Minnie the Moocher' and 'Kicking the Gong Around', Lew would announce that he was going to try out some new vocalists in the band, and Ernie Ritte, Alfie Noakes and Lew Davis would all come downstage to the mike and sing a chorus each in turn of 'Lying in the Hay'. In the middle of this, a terrible coughing would be heard and although Lew Davis seemed to continue singing, no sound could be heard. All would be revealed when the voice resumed and it was seen that Al Bowlly had been ghosting for the crooners all the time, using another mike attached to his guitar, After another Nat Gonella vocal, 'Let Him Live', it would be time for the last number: 'I Cover the Waterfront' sung by Al Bowlly, with the whole front line coming forward in a V-formation, and playing the last chorus *pianissimo*. The curtain would drop slowly, to riotous applause.

For two sisters from Dulwich, who were in the audience one night, this was the greatest moment of their lives. Hilda and Lesley Harding were devoted Tuesday night listeners. Each week, they would invite their friends round to their house in Landells Road to listen to The Monseigneur broadcast. They would roll up the carpet and push back the chairs and, with Mum and Dad watching from the sofa, they would dance their way through the programme. To see Al Bowlly in person had been their dream and at the Holborn Empire it came true. After the show, they went round to the stage door in the hopes of catching a glimpse of their hero. They saw him and even spoke to him. 'We were in seventh heaven!' remembers Hilda. 'When you're young and you look up to someone like that, the idea of meeting him is out of this world. He was very kind to us. Very gentle, very friendly. It was as if this wasn't the first time we were speaking to him, but that we'd known him all our lives. He made us feel completely at ease. He even invited us round to his flat!'

The girls went backstage again, after a show at the Alhambra theatre. This time they had a present for Al—hand-stitched underpants, which they'd secretly run up at the clothing manufacturers where they both worked. He was delighted, and took the girls home to meet Marjie. Soon she, too, was receiving hand-made undies. Al was also responsible for the girls' first real glimpse of West End night life. 'He met us in the Haymarket, and he said, "You're always on the outside looking in—come inside for a change." So he fixed us up with a table on the balcony in the Kit-Kat, and we watched the dancing.'

The remarkable thing about the Harding sisters' friendship with Al was that there was never any sense of 'he's the star, we're the fans'. It seemed altogether natural for Al to meet his listeners, to invite them round to his place (with no ulterior motive), and to become friends with them. Once when their radio was being repaired, he let them listen to The Monseigneur broadcast in his flat. 'We locked up and came away before he got back—we had to catch the last tram home.' He also rescued them from an embarrassing situation in Lyons Corner House, when they found themselves unable to pay the bill. 'We had awful visions of doing the washing-up for the rest of the day, so we went round to Cranbourne Mansions, fished Al Bowlly out, and he gave us a ten-bob note with which to pay the bill.' The sisters also met Al Bowlly's mother, who came over from Johannesburg for a holiday. 'She was a very sweet old lady. Very, very old. Very dark-skinned, much darker than Al was.'

Shortly after his mother's visit, Al moved from Cranbourne Mansions to a new flat at 17 Orange Street, Piccadilly. It was

there that he was interviewed by *Melody Maker*; the reporter, Miles Henslow, came away with a photograph of Al singing in his bath, and a recorded conversation that revealed Al's single-minded dedication to his art: 'Well, Mr Bowlly,' he began, 'what is your favourite occupation?'—'Singing.'
'I mean when you are at home?'—'Singing.'
'Haven't you a hobby?'—'Singing.'
Al Bowlly, concluded Henslow, was essentially a singer.

Champagne and Strawberries

'With his lips a bare three inches from the microphone, he sings softly, confidently—and more people thrill to his voice than to Mussolini's and Hitler's put together.' Al Bowlly in 1933—a description not from the musical press, but from the fashionable London magazine *Ideas*. Bowlly's fame was now spreading beyond the ranks of dance music devotees; he was en route to becoming a national celebrity. He was to be seen, briefly, in several Elstree movies: with Anna Neagle in *The Little Damozell* and *Bittersweet*; with Sydney Howard and Claude Hulbert in *The Mayor's Nest*. He played the part of George the tramp in *The Mayor's Nest*; in his big scene, he sang 'The Wedding of the Slumtown Babes', sitting on a doorstep while a gang of children acted out the lines of the song.

Occasionally, a critical voice was raised against the 'crooners', and their microphone-orientated, *sotto voce* singing style. *Punch* railed against Bowlly and his kind, and coined the word 'croonitis' to describe the disease that was spreading across the land, transmitted by radio. In reply, Al Bowlly made a recording of 'Glorious Devon' which he sang 'straight'—while on the reverse side Owen Bryngwyn, tenor, turned crooner to sing 'Let's Put out the Lights'. Honours remained more or less even.

In May week, Al Bowlly sang at two Cambridge May Balls: the first with Ray Noble's band, the second with Lew Stone. The music critic of *Granta*, the university magazine, took the opportunity to make a critical comparison of the two bands:

> Lew Stone is the victim of two evil influences. The first is the one which attacks nearly every dance musician in this country, with the glaring exception of Ray Noble; it is an attempt to

copy the idiom of construction employed by the leading negro bands. Lew Stone is also an exponent of the dotted quaver eight-in-a-bar slow foxtrot rhythm which comes, I believe, from the pernicious source of Leo Reisman. He is, in fact, a victim of the fashionable melodic rhythm of the moment. Ray Noble is probably as different from Lew Stone as any arranger in England today. If he errs anywhere it is on the side of over-orchestration, although his recent record of 'What a Perfect Combination' has proved him to be an arranger capable of producing arrangements in the same idiom as Stone, but of a style greatly superior. His arrangements are always well balanced and constructed and for the most part, simple. Ray Noble's and Lew Stone's records of 'Won't You Stay to Tea?' form a very interesting comparison.

The musicians refused to be drawn into these erudite comparative analyses. They were more concerned with the backstage facilities, or lack of them. 'We used to have bottles of champagne given to us', complains Tiny Winters, 'and we didn't want any part of it. All we wanted was a cup of tea. But it was like gold-dust—you had no chance of getting a cup of tea in those places. Because there were no facilities, you see, for making tea. Sometimes we'd be put in one of the students' rooms—a tiny room in the college—and that was the bandroom where we had to change and everything. The champagne was no use to us, because we weren't drinkers. Al Bowlly was one of those people who just can't take it. Alcohol seemed to disagree with him; if he had one or two whiskies it did something to his stomach and made him irritable. So he very rarely touched the stuff.'

That May Week engagement was the very first 'live' appearance of the Ray Noble Orchestra, which had been playing together for nearly two and a half years—but only in the HMV recording studio. The fact that most of Ray Noble's musicians were also playing in Lew Stone's band at The Monseigneur made it almost impossible for Ray Noble to accept evening bookings. However, in the summer of 1933, when The Monseigneur closed for six weeks, Ray Noble was able to organize a band to go to Holland, to play at a seaside resort near the Hague called

Scheveningen. 'We had four weeks of hard work and jollity,' recalls Nat Gonella, 'so much so that when we got back to England, I had to spend the next two weeks in a nursing home, recuperating from the four weeks in Holland!' The band included Tiny Winters, Harry Berly, Bill Harty, Lew Davis, Alfie Noakes, Freddie Gardner, and Al Bowlly. Several of the musicians brought their wives with them on this 'busman's holiday'. Al Bowlly brought his girlfriend Marjie. Ray Noble is very proud of the fact that they were one of the first bands to travel by charter plane.

> KLM provided all the facilities, but at the last moment when they saw how much gear we had, they said they couldn't possibly fit us all on the plane. I said it was a bit late to tell us that, so they agreed to put on a second plane with all the baggage. Then we had to get clearance permits for everything. My wife got all the papers together, and we arrived at Rotterdam airport with a great big box full of papers. When we showed them the box, they said 'No, we don't need papers, we need photographs.' So we took photographs. We took every kind of a photograph you could think of. *Then* they said they wanted to see the papers. It was just a lot of nonsense, really. You could have thrown them into the sea. But we had a very pleasant time there.

Scheveningen was the premier resort in the Netherlands, the Dutch equivalent of Brighton. Miles of sandy beaches and beautiful hotels. Holidaymakers came from France and Germany, but there were not many English. So the Ray Noble band was instructed to wave the flag, and to be on their best behaviour. 'They were the only people to play on the beach,' recalls Ray Noble. 'They made pyramids, and fell all over the place—and actually went in the water and swam!' The band stayed at the Palace Hotel. There were absolutely no complaints about the catering or accommodation: the musicians were treated as royalty. Al Bowlly shared a honeymoon suite with Marjie, who was travelling as his wife (although legally he was still married to Freda Roberts at that time). Meals were taken in the hotel dining room, alongside the customers. Nat Gonella remembers that they used to 'drink champagne and strawberries from a big bowl. That was sort of ad lib or "*à la carte*"!' Al Bowlly revealed a predilection for ginger, according to Lew Davis: 'It was served as a dessert, in some sort of liquid. I thought it was horrible. But Al got the waiters to serve a tremendous portion to him, and after every single meal! One day Marjie said to him "Al, let me taste a bit." He said, "Don't you embarrass me—don't you take any of my ginger." And he covered the ginger with his two hands, and wouldn't let anybody touch it. When he'd finished on this particular day, because it was an extra large portion, he was absolutely dripping with perspiration—it just poured off him.'

The band played in the Kurhaus, the monumental Palace of Fun which still dominates the Scheveningen promenade. Every afternoon, from 3.30 to 5.30, they played on the terrace for tea-dances. In the evening, they moved indoors to the massive ballroom, where they played from 9.00 until midnight. Apart from a few last-minute arrangements, the band mostly played reduced versions of their established record numbers. 'We didn't need a very large book,' says Ray Noble. 'They only wanted to hear the particular tunes they already knew from our records.' Al Bowlly did all the vocals; the comic croakings of Nat Gonella and Tiny Winters, which Lew Stone had encouraged, were out of keeping with Ray Noble's smooth, elegant brand of dance music. 'What More Can I Ask?', 'The Very Thought of You', and 'Goodnight Sweetheart' were Al's most requested numbers. The atmosphere was relaxed and friendly.

A certain amount of fraternization between musicians and patrons—which was never allowed in The Monseigneur—flourished in the Kurhaus: the band played with one eye on their music, and the other on the dance-floor, talent-spotting. Ray Noble recalls:

> One night we were playing away, when a beautiful girl made an entrance. She must have been about twenty-two, part-Javanese, and part-Dutch. She walked into the room quite quietly, with her escort, and crossed the floor to her table. And the whole band stopped playing! It's the only time I've ever known a band stop like that, because she was the most beautiful

thing we'd ever seen in our lives. She was unspeakably glorious —her skin colour glowed. And we missed four beats: the only person who kept going was the drummer Bill Harty, because he wasn't looking at the time. He was bending down trying to pick up a drum stick, and so we just had his bass drum going for about four beats—bom, bom, bom, bom! And then the band said, 'Oh God' and picked it up again . . . It was an extraordinary moment.

In the first week of September, Ray Noble and his musicians returned to London, and went their separate ways. Nat Gonella went to a health farm, to recover from his exertions. Al Bowlly re-opened his Orange Street flat, and went back to work. On 11 September, *Melody Maker* reported an extraordinary scene in Holborn: 'Fully half an hour after the Holborn Empire had closed, a mob of a hundred or more people, mostly women, besieged Al Bowlly for his autograph around a sand-bin on which he had to write autographs. He had just enjoyed a personal triumph on the stage, where he appeared for the first time as a solo artist.'

Accompanied by his friend Monia Liter on the piano, Al had put together a programme of his favourite songs. He opened with 'Some of these Days'; then he sang 'Learn to Croon' and 'I Cover the Waterfront', during which the audience in the first few rows could clearly see that there were tears in his eyes. There were problems with his microphone, which was making strange noises. He replaced it with another, and then sang 'Minnie the Moocher', '*A Brivele der Mame*' and 'If You were the Only Girl in the World'. His inexperience of stagecraft showed itself here, when, without looking at what he was doing, he put out a hand to support himself on the piano, missed it, and fell over backwards. He recovered for his signing-off tune, 'Some of These Days', after which he came out in front of the tabs to sing 'Brother, Can You Spare a Dime?', in a strange-looking ragged Norfolk jacket.

'Making all allowances for his obvious anxiety to please on this, his first solo variety date,' said *Melody Maker*, 'he did enough to prove that he is a great draw and a real top-liner. Had he been better served with more efficient mikes, he would undoubtedly have sung to even greater effect. He certainly has no peer among British crooners.'

Two days later, Al Bowlly was back in the Lew Stone Band for the opening night of the new season at The Monseigneur Restaurant. After their summer adventures by the sea, the musicians were happy to be back in the familiar, exclusive luxury of the West End. 'I sometimes feel sorry for young musicians of today, who've never known that sort of gay, carefree atmosphere,' said Joe Crossman of The Monseigneur days. 'It was such a comfortable, elegant place. The sound was good—the acoustics were great. And everybody who came in seemed to know the band. It was like a big party, every night of the week.'

But the party was coming to an end. Jack Upson had lost interest in the restaurant business and offered The Monseigneur building for sale to a syndicate of which bandleader Jack Harris was a member. Harris, who until then had led a band at the Café de Paris, prevailed upon his business partners to let him move to The Monseigneur: in exchange, Lew Stone was given first refusal of the Café de Paris vacancy. In the event, he preferred to take his band to the Café Anglais, which was owned by the same management. He chose to go to the Anglais because of its better facilities for broadcasting: Harry Roy had broadcast regularly from there, before he switched to the Mayfair. To complete the shuffle, Roy Fox now moved into the Café de Paris. By December, the three bands were installed in their new positions. But the game of musical chairs was not yet over. The sale of The Monseigneur miscarried, and Upson found himself, reluctantly, still in control of the restaurant but without his friend Lew Stone on the bandstand. There were disagreements with the incumbent Jack Harris, who now found himself cast as employee, rather than proprietor. Soon it became clear that a further re-shuffle was inevitable. Harris was reluctant to return to the Café Anglais and he had set his sights on the more prestigious Café de Paris, but Fox refused to move out. There was no question of Lew Stone going to the Café de Paris; Upson wanted him back at The Monseigneur. A compromise was reached, and in April 1934, Lew Stone re-opened at The Monseigneur, while Jack Harris took his band to the Café de Paris, to play alternate sessions with

Roy Fox. 'Personally, I shall be happy to have Jack Harris here,' said Roy. 'There is room for both of us.'

Throughout all this, Lew Stone had cannily contrived to hang on to his Tuesday night radio slot, and thereby retained his dominant hold on the listening audience. The manœuvres also gave him an opportunity to take his band on the road again: first in the London suburbs and then, in early 1934, to the provinces. In London, they played a week at the Palladium where, for the first time, Al Bowlly was seen to be using a portable hand-mike. After a tour of Moss Empires—Finsbury Park, Stratford, Shepherds Bush, Streatham—they headed north, and the enthusiastic response of their London audiences was now totally overshadowed by the near-riots that greeted them there. Manchester, Bradford, York—'It was a big hall but I think there were nearly 5,000 people there,' remembers Nat Gonella. 'And from playing in theatres and cinemas, it was quite a jump to see all these people more or less free to come and touch you or knock you about. It was a bit frightening.' Edinburgh, Glasgow, Birmingham, Nottingham—'We broke the record there,' says Tiny Winters. 'People were scrambling for autographs—it really did bring home to us what people felt about the band.' Bristol, Southampton, Portsmouth—'Huge crowds, nearly all women,' recalls Nat Gonella's then future wife, Dorothy, who was in the audience at Portsmouth. 'And when Al Bowlly came on, the place was in an uproar. Because it was the first time we'd ever seen him. I'd imagined he was going to be taller—he was quite short. But we thought he was lovely.' When the band played in ballrooms, nobody danced. They stood ten-deep in front of the bandstand. In the intermission, Al would sit at a table signing autographs; the queue would go all round the hall. In Bradford, Al left the stage during an instrumental number, and was besieged by girls. He couldn't fight his way back to the rostrum in time for his next vocal and the band was left to fill in for thirty-two bars.

The Lew Stone band coasted back to London on a wave of popular adulation. Even the unassuming Al Bowlly was beginning to bask in the euphoria of success. 'He used to walk just a little bit straighter,' says Nat, 'and I think he put half an inch on the heels of his shoes!' The band's triumphal tour of Britain's dance-halls had synchronized with a series of personal triumphs for Al Bowlly, who lived up to his reputation as 'Joe Sex' in hotel bedrooms, dressing rooms, bandrooms—even, at the Birmingham Palais, in the gent's cloakroom during an intermission. There was nothing devious or underhand about these encounters: Al found it natural to accept what was freely offered to him by his enthusiastic admirers, the dance band equivalents of rock music's 'groupies'. It's almost as if he saw this as the inevitable culmination of his relationship with his audience—a loving relationship, which found its perfect expression in the lyrics that only he could sing with real emotion, and genuine sentiment.

In the *Bristol Evening Post*'s edition of 12 April 1934, there is a photograph of Al singing to an audience of 3,000 at the Bristol Coliseum. Taken from behind the band, it shows a beautifully-groomed Al Bowlly singing into an ornate microphone, with an expression of blissful happiness on his face. At his side, facing the band, stands the solid, reassuring figure of his mentor, Lew Stone. Below the stage is a sea of smiling faces. The photograph captures the supreme moment of a perfect connection between the singer and his audience. Appropriately, the song that stopped the show that night was 'Everything I Have is Yours':

> Everything I have is yours:
> You're part of me.
> Everything I have is yours:
> You're my destiny.
> Everything that I possess
> I offer you
> Let my dream of happiness
> Come true . . .

Even at this high point in his career, there remained for Al Bowlly one dream unrealized, one ambition unfulfilled. For musicians in the 'thirties, the 'Golden Light in the West' was the heartland of jazz—New York. To get there was the ultimate aspiration: to *play* there was the stuff of dreams. Imagine, therefore, Al's excitement when, in the summer of 1934, Ray Noble approached him with the news that he'd had an offer from America. There were, in fact, two offers, both of them attractive. The Rockwell

O'Keefe Bureau wanted him to lead his orchestra at the famous Rainbow Room in New York, and another band agency, this one the biggest of them all, the Music Corporation of America, wanted him as musical director on a radio programme, sponsored by the makers of Bromo-Seltzer, America's favourite hangover cure.

All this transatlantic activity was a direct result of Noble's New Mayfair Orchestra recordings for HMV. Ray himself explained: 'HMV at that time had an arrangement with the Victor Company in New York for an interchange of masters. And so a lot of our stuff was getting a lot of sales, particularly in the colleges. The agents began to get interested in the bloke who makes the records.'

It is impossible to exaggerate the excitement that the American interest in Ray Noble generated among British musicians. With the exception of Jack Hylton, whose lively comedy numbers and Whitemanesque concert arrangements were being released on record in the States and going down well, Ray was the only British dance-band leader in whom the Americans had shown the slightest interest. To have received two offers almost simultaneously was the ultimate accolade. Most flattering of all was the opinion of American musicians themselves, here expressed by George T. Simon, who was editor-in-chief of *Metronome*, a prestigious New York music magazine, for sixteen years. Simon described Noble's records as 'exquisitely played and excellently recorded', a resounding compliment to his musicianship and to the quality of the engineering at HMV's Abbey Road studios.

The Rockwell O'Keefe Bureau (which was also the booking agency for the Dorsey Brothers) had wanted to bring Noble's band over intact, but they met with two major difficulties: one, that the American Musicians' Union wouldn't stand for it, and, two, that Ray Noble didn't have a band of his own anyway, and had merely assembled top musicians from various English bands for his recordings. 'Not to worry,' said Tommy Rockwell. 'We'll organize a band of American musicians for him. But we would like that singer he uses on the records—what's his name? Al Bowlly.'

Ray happily agreed and the deal was made. In addition to Al, he decided to take Bill Harty, the dapper little drummer who had played both with Lew Stone at The Monseigneur and on the New Mayfair Orchestra recordings. Bill would accompany him not as a drummer, but as his personal manager. 'Bill Harty had already been in the States and knew the area there, so if I took Bill I had somebody who could talk to musicians. And I had to bring Al because he was associated with us, and people wanted to hear you play in person what they had heard on the records.' There remained the question of existing contracts, Ray's with HMV, Al's and Bill Harty's with Lew Stone. Louis Sterling, head of HMV and himself an American, urged Ray to go, and offered to keep his job open for a year. 'Couldn't be nicer than that', says Ray. Lew Stone, with characteristic generosity, put no obstacle in the way of the departure of two of his key men.

There was never any doubt about Al's reaction. A phone call came early one morning, and the caretaker called up from the hall: 'It's Mr Noble. He wants to know if you'll go to New York with him.' Would he? He'd like to see somebody try to stop him! This was the break he had long been waiting for. On 11 August 1934, *Melody Maker* reported the event:

> After a career in England that has been as colourful and as successful as any musician in years, one of our greatest vocalists is joining up with Ray Noble when the latter embarks in a few weeks' time on the greatest adventure of his life—practically emigration to America. This is Al Bowlly, crooner-in-chief to Lew Stone. When Lew returns to work at The Monseigneur next September, Al will not be with him, but on his way over the Atlantic to fresh triumphs, maybe, on the boards and on the mikes of the new world—new vistas for a singer from Mozambique who was once told by a Johannesburg café proprietor to 'quit that awful noise'.

Sixty-five Stories Nearer the Stars

'All-powerful and omnipotent—the strongest trade union in the world', was how *Melody Maker* described the American Federation of Musicians. A little over the top perhaps, but not by much. American musicians did indeed have a formidable organization to guard their interests. Not only did the AFM protect them against predatory employers and foreign intruders, it even protected them from themselves. If a New York musician wished to move west in order to share the lush pickings in the booming film studios, he would have to cool his heels for six months establishing Los Angeles residency before he was allowed to blow a dollar-earning note. British musicians, with their ramshackle and impotent Musicians Union, could only regard their colleagues across the Atlantic with awe and envy.

Even before he left England, and despite his firm contracts, Ray Noble heard of trouble brewing in New York. At the beginning of September Bill Harty was hastily sent on ahead to negotiate. On the 8th, *Melody Maker* reported:

> The attempted ban on Noble, instigated by the American labour authorities, is a direct outcome of a howl of protest by the Executive Committee of the American Federation of Musicians . . . Two well-known American bandleaders lodged strong protests with the Federation against Noble being allowed to enter America, even though, in order to comply with all the temperamental prejudices of the American musicians, Noble and his sponsors, the Rockwell O'Keefe Bureau, had agreed that the band behind him, with the exception of Al Bowlly, should be one hundred per cent American. It was feared that to permit Ray Noble to come to America—the first British dance-band leader to do so—would set a precedent that

might result in a veritable flood of British musicians into the United States.

This latest example of Yankee xenophobia drew hollow laughter from the British. What about the 'veritable flood' of *American* musicians into the United Kingdom? That flood had been running merrily ever since The Original Dixieland Jazz Band had landed in 1919. Jack Hylton, the only British band leader other than Ray Noble whose recordings had led to American offers, returned from fruitless meetings with the implacable AFM and whimsically told a *Melody Maker* representative of a dream he'd had on the voyage. Conducting the first night of a New York engagement, his downbeat had been greeted by a most extraordinary noise from the band. Amazed and terrified, he saw before him 'not the famous Hyltonians, but, in the sax section, Danny Polo, Howard Jacobs, Abe Aronsohn and Coleman Hawkins; Louis Armstrong and Roy Fox on trumpets, Jack Harris on violin, and Carroll Gibbons and Charlie Kunz on two pianos.' All, of course, American musicians, welcome and working in London.

With his future still in doubt, Ray Noble left for New York, and a few days later, in mid-October, Al Bowlly and Marjie sailed from Plymouth aboard the *Ile de France*. His departure caused some anguish. Maurice Elwin, a singer who billed himself as 'Monarch of the Microphone', wrote in the music magazine *Rhythm*: 'Instead of being glad that Al Bowlly is going to America, I feel sorry about it. It seems such a great pity to allow a potential box office colossus to slip through the fingers of British showmen . . . I wait patiently to see how much it will cost us to bring him back to this country after he has been correctly exploited in America.'

In New York, the AFM held its ground. Ray Noble was not to be permitted to open at the Rainbow Room. There were discussions about his coaching and arranging for the orchestra which would then be led by an American bandleader; there was even a suggestion that he go to Toronto, form a band of Canadian musicians and broadcast to the United States from there. Ray rejected all of this for the nonsense it clearly was. What seems to have aroused the Federation's resentment most was the fact that Ray had undertaken several engagements concurrently—which of course was the very reason for his accepting the deal in the first place.

For Al Bowlly, prospects were brighter. As a singer, he could be regarded as an entertainer and (provided he didn't touch his guitar) not as a musician, and was therefore free to accept whatever engagements might come his way. Almost immediately upon his arrival in New York, Bill Harty was able to cable *Melody Maker* in London with the news that 'Al Bowlly has signed a big long-term radio contract with NBC.' The contract was, in fact, for the very same radio show that Ray Noble was being prevented from doing—*The Bromo-Seltzer Hour*, which was now to feature the orchestra of Victor Young, a distinguished musician, famous for his work with the top singers, and composer of such hit songs as 'Sweet Sue, Just You', 'A Ghost Of A Chance' and 'A Hundred Years From Today'. Later Young was to write a very big hit indeed—the title song for the film *Around the World in Eighty Days*.

At last, on 20 October, *Melody Maker* was able to report that Ray Noble had 'won out of a situation of amazing difficulty, national insularity and unredeemed promises'. He was now in Hollywood, composing songs and arranging the music for Paramount's *Big Broadcast of 1936*. There was better news still to come. Under pressure from Tommy Rockwell of Rockwell O'Keefe, helped by the intrepid Bill Harty, the AFM had finally agreed that Ray Noble was free to appear in New York conducting an orchestra and that the Rainbow Room engagement would begin as soon as he returned from the Coast.

Meanwhile Al and Marjie had set themselves up in a modest suite at the Abbey-Victoria Hotel on Seventh Avenue and 51st Street, just a stone's throw from Broadway, and were beginning to get to know the fabulous city that was to be their home. First, however, they had to come to terms with the cost of living in New York. They discovered, for instance, that in the hotel all extras had to be paid for in cash—dry cleaning, laundry, even a cup of coffee. And every time you called room service, that meant another tip. Later, Al was to write: 'Within ten days of our arrival I realized I was actually spending sixty dollars a week more than I was earning.'

But Al was never the one to allow a little thing like shortage of cash to interfere with his enjoyment of life. He quickly made friends with the hospitable and warm-hearted New Yorkers, and soon he and Marjie were being entertained all around the town. He was introduced to American sporting events and fast became addicted to football and to the ice hockey played at Madison Square Garden. And he had plenty of work. There was the weekly radio show to do, and by November he had recorded four titles with Victor Young: 'If I Had A Million Dollars', 'Be Still, My Heart', 'Say When' and 'When Love Comes Swingin' Along'. Al enjoyed both the work and the play. But the best was yet to come—the opening night of Ray Noble and his Orchestra at the Rainbow Room.

As soon as the Rockwell O'Keefe agency had decided that Ray should have an American band behind him at the Rainbow Room, they had looked around for someone to organize it for him. There was no need to look far. The man they chose had performed the same service for one of their most important clients—the Dorsey Brothers Orchestra. His name was Glenn Miller. Five years later Glenn Miller was to become the most famous bandleader in the history of dance music; in 1935 he was a respected and influential trombonist arranger, much in demand around the name bands and in the recording studios of New York City. He set about putting together a band for Ray Noble. George Simon, in his fine book *Glenn Miller*, takes up the story: 'And what a band Glenn organized! Charlie Spivak and Pee Wee Irwin played trumpets; Glenn and Wilbur Schwitzenberg, who later changed his name to Will Bradley, were on trombones; the reeds featured Bud Freeman and Johnny Mince, who later was to star as clarinettist in Tommy Dorsey's band; and the rhythm section consisted of Claude Thornhill on piano, the brilliant George Van Eps on guitar, Delmar Kaplan on bass, and Noble's manager, Bill Harty, a not very swinging drummer, who had arrived with Ray from England.' Bill Harty had never expected to be allowed to play his drums, but there he was in the band. Simon's unkind aside about 'a not very swinging drummer' merely underlines the gulf which, in the mid-'thirties, separated the playing of British and American instrumentalists. Be that as it may, Will Bradley once remarked, 'The rhythm section didn't sound as bad as Harty was capable of playing.'

In addition to the four brass, four saxes, four rhythm line-up, there were also three violinists: Fritz Prospero, Nick Pisani and Danny D'Andrea. And of course, there was the singer, Al Bowlly. As George Simon had observed: 'What a band.' Later, four of its members were themselves to become leaders of successful bands: Will Bradley, Charlie Spivak, Claude Thornhill and the incomparable Glenn Miller.

While Ray Noble was in Hollywood, working on *The Big Broadcast*, Glenn Miller rehearsed the band and moulded it to his tastes. George Simon comments: 'That was fine, too, with many of the jazz-orientated musicians he had assembled for a leader whose bag was sweet stuff. When Ray returned from the West Coast, he took over, concentrating on ballads. Both he and Glenn were sticklers for musical details, so the band spent an inordinate amount of time just rehearsing, for which the men were paid—"the first time in history", according to [Bud] Freeman, "that this ever happened".'

Ray Noble had enjoyed his Hollywood stint. *The Big Broadcast of 1936* was a follow-up to the 1932 film which had launched Bing Crosby upon his spectacular career with such songs as 'Please', and his theme song, 'When The Blue Of The Night Meets The Gold Of The Day'. The 1936 edition again featured Bing, now a fully fledged star, along with Jack Oakie, Amos 'n' Andy, Ethel Merman and Burns and Allen. Ray's meeting with George and Gracie was to have an important effect upon his future. He conducted a West Coast orchestra in the film, and composed one of its songs: 'Why Stars Come Out At Night'. When shooting was over, Ray hurried back to New York.

The Rainbow Room, 'sixty-five stories nearer the stars', as the radio announcers used to say, was possibly the smartest dining and dancing spot in New York City. It occupied the top floor of the RCA building in Radio City, a vast complex spread over no less than four city blocks between Fifth and Sixth Avenues. The cover charge at the Rainbow Room (the cost merely to sit at one of its tables) was twenty-five dollars, a vast sum in those days; and if the eagle eye of the *maître d'hôtel* didn't guarantee the exclusiveness of the clientele, then the size of the bill most certainly did.

The band played from Monday to Saturday from 9.00 pm until 3.00 am. There was a floor show to be accompanied, and a weekly broadcast. Ray Noble is reputed to have been paid £450 a week, and the boys in the band were also earning good money. It was hard work but enjoyable. George Simon writes: 'Everything pointed to this becoming one of the great all-round bands of all time. And for a while it proved to be just that. Noble, suave and sophisticated, arranged ballads with great musical taste and tenderness. His English band's jazz efforts had often bordered on the comical. Now, with the jazz-wise Miller to take over that department, the band appeared to have all bases well covered.'

The band played Ray Noble's immaculate music and the well-dressed, well-heeled dancers loved it. They were, Ray remembers, a fussy and knowledgeable crowd: 'I mean, it's remarkable to think that you could have a bank president who'd say, "You haven't played that number I like so much. I have a record of it at home." You'd play it and he'd say, "It doesn't sound the same." And you'd say, "Well we used something on the record that we can't reproduce in the room." In those days, people knew about these things.'

As the evening turned into morning, the dinner-dancers would depart, and the college crowd would arrive; the West Pointers and the Annapolis kids, the students from Yale and Harvard with their pretty girlfriends. It was then that the band would show off its jazz soloists: Johnny Mince, Claude Thornhill, George Van Eps and especially Bud Freeman, 'whose wild inventive solos', says Simon, 'created all sorts of excitement.'

Al sat on the bandstand and took care of the ballads. The customers at the Rainbow Room loved his easy and fluent style of singing and his ready smile. He got along with everybody, both on the stand and in front of it. George Simon says: 'One of the nicest gents I ever met was Al Bowlly, whose warm and tender phrasing was a true reflection of his personality . . . One of my fondest memories is of Bowlly taking me aside and telling me he'd like to sing me a song that Glenn had just written. Actually, only the melody was Glenn's; the lyrics were by Eddie Heyman, best known as the lyricist of "Body And Soul". Al was a very sentimental guy who had no trouble showing his emotions, and I thought he was actually going to cry as he sang, without any accompaniment, the new song he had just learned and which obviously had affected him very much, Later the song was given a new set of lyrics when it was retitled "Moonlight Serenade", but who remembers the words? Yet, ever since I first heard them, I've been unable to forget the original lyrics of "Now I Lay Me Down To Weep", as Al Bowlly crooned them just for me that early morning in the band's dressing room:

> Weep for the moon, for the moon has no reason to glow now;
> Weep for the rose, for the rose had no reason to grow now;
> The river won't flow now,
> As I lay me down to weep.

... It was never published until it became "Moonlight Serenade", and was never recorded by any band—even Noble's—until Glenn's own band did it four years later.'

Ray Noble and his Orchestra broadcast regularly from the Rainbow Room, over the NCB network, coast to coast. A look at some of the numbers, with vocals by Al Bowlly, which the band recorded on the Victor label in the first half of 1935 will give some idea of what American listeners were hearing on their radios: 'Soon', 'Down By The River', 'My Melancholy Baby', 'Top Hat', 'The Piccolino', 'I Wished On The Moon', and Ray's own tune, 'Why Stars Come Out At Night'. 'Way Down Yonder In New Orleans' had a Glenn Miller arrangement complete with the repeated rhythmic riffs that Glenn always liked to feature.

In America, just as in England, a regular spot on the air was the key to nationwide popularity. Al was amazed when he discovered just how powerful radio could be. Rudy Vallee, the man who had practically invented crooning back in 1925, and who had become a good friend, showed Al some of the letters he had received after one broadcast. 'It was not uncommon', said Al, 'for him to receive 75,000 pieces of fan mail following each broadcast. And, in addition, a barrage of telephone calls from his admirers immediately following each programme. I was filled with envy when Rudy showed me the well organized office he maintained just to deal with his radio fans. But within ten days of opening at the Rainbow Room and broadcasting on network radio, I had the happy experience of seeing the same type of fan mail staff, and phone operators frenziedly busy handling the incoming enquiries about the "new British singer".' One of Al's favourite fan letters came from a girl, who wrote: 'When your voice comes on the air, it's just like fizzy lemonade being poured down my spine!'

There could be no possible doubt about the success of 'the new British singer'. For Victor, Al recorded four songs with accompaniment by Ray Noble and his Orchestra: 'You And The Night And The Music', 'Blue Room', 'In A Blue And Pensive Mood' and 'A Little White Gardenia'. For a mere band singer to be awarded four solo records was almost without precedent. Autograph-hunters assembled nightly to greet his arrival at Radio City, and a hardy few were still there when he left at 3.00 am. Al was fond of telling a story about the occasion when he turned up for work with only minutes to spare and hurriedly signed a few autograph albums. About to sign on a sheet of paper thrust at him from the crowd, he noticed that it was folded back at the top. Curious to discover why, he unfolded it, and read, above the space where he would have signed: 'Please pay the bearer the sum of eight thousand dollars.' It was addressed to Al's bank!

There was the nightly stint at the Rainbow Room, almost daily rehearsals, a weekly meeting to choose songs, set keys and work out routines. On top of all this, Ray had also acquired a weekly half-hour radio show for Coty Cosmetics, and that meant a long hard day in the studios. And as if all that were not enough, Al signed personally with NBC for thirty-six half-hours with the orchestra of Al Goodman, a great favourite with radio audiences at that time. It was a busy but exciting life.

Only Sundays were absolutely free. 'Sometimes', Ray Noble recalls, 'we'd make a little party and we'd go out—Al and Marjie, my wife and I, Bill Harty and his wife. We'd go to Jack

Dempsey's restaurant and then to Madison Square Garden to see the ice hockey. Al was a real sports fan. Bill and I always had Al sit between us because if the umpire made a decision he didn't like, he'd want to go down there and kill him. He'd leap to his feet, the veins would come out on his head and we'd have to hold on to him in case he had a heart attack, or something. Al was a most excitable man.'

In 1936, Ray Noble went on tour. Success on radio, on records and at the Rainbow Room had turned the band into a major attraction. 'We went up to Vermont, almost to the Canadian border,' recalls Ray. 'Then we went South, right down to Texas. We played one-night stands, college dances, and movie theatres where we did five shows a day. At the Paramount in New York we did seven shows a day at the weekend, and that is practically living in the dark, all the time.' They worked hard, but as a big-time band they did it in style. When trains couldn't be relied upon for a long and complicated journey, they travelled in an air-conditioned bus, something new for those days. The married men established their wives in comfortable hotels while they toured the neighbouring towns, and it was during this period that Al and Marjie were married.

Ray Noble recalls that 'It was something to do with visas.' More likely it was because some western and southern states with less liberal laws than those in force in New York or California did not take too kindly to couples living together without the benefit of clergy. The Nobles made all the arrangements and put on a little wedding celebration.

They were good for each other, Al and Marjie. Of course, Marjie had no illusions about the man she had married. She knew that Al, a famous singer with a famous band, would continue to have a great many feminine admirers; that not only were they important to his career, they were also an essential prop to his self-esteem. And she knew that if their marriage was to succeed, she would just have to learn to live with it.

Once, in Boston, as Al left rehearsal one morning, he was recognized by some girls from a nearby factory which was disgorging itself for the lunch time break. Before he could make his escape, he was surrounded by his delighted fans, all shrieking and screaming and attempting, if possible, to obtain some souvenir of his clothing. Some even produced scissors and tried to snip off locks of his hair. Under the onslaught, Al's braces gave way, and he was frantically trying to hold up his trousers with one hand, and ward off those lethal scissors with the other. When the police arrived and rescued him, his clothes were torn to shreds and his face was covered with lipstick.

Ray Noble adds: 'Al had an enormous fascination for women, and with his simple nature he took what came along. But it doesn't necessarily mean that he was constantly at war with his wife. He always came back to her and often admitted his faults quite openly. When they had quarrels they were fierce. Marjie would grab something and say, "You come near me and I'll hit you with this!" And Al would take off his belt and say, "I'll whip you within an inch of your life!" Twenty minutes later he'd be crying in her lap and swearing never to leave her again. He had a lovable, simple nature.' Marjie was clearly a very understanding lady. Al once gave her a love letter from a broken-hearted hat-check girl, and asked her to please write to the girl and give her the brush off.

In August 1936, the Nobles and the Bowllys came back to England for a holiday and to do some recording for HMV. They made a Ray Noble Medley and Al sang choruses of Ray's lovely songs, 'The Touch Of Your Lips' and 'Goodnight Sweetheart'.

Then it was back to the States, to the Rainbow Room and more recording and broadcasting. Among the titles Al recorded in September and October were 'Easy To Love', 'I've Got You Under My Skin', 'One, Two, Button My Shoe', 'Little Old Lady' and 'There's Something In The Air'. But things weren't going quite as well as they had gone the previous year. The contract for the Coty Cosmetics radio show was not renewed, and when another theatre tour was proposed and the boys were asked to take a cut in salary, some of the star players decided that the time had come to move on. Johnny Mince followed Pee Wee Irwin into the new Tommy Dorsey Orchestra, and Glenn Miller left to resume his efforts to create his own band.

Incidentally, Miller's sojourn with Ray Noble's orchestra is not without its interest to jazz historians. For it was while playing second trombone for Ray that he had encountered, purely by accident, what was soon to be celebrated the world over as 'The Miller Sound'. Glenn Miller explained it all in an interview he gave to *Metronome* magazine: 'Pee Wee Irwin, now playing trumpet for Tommy Dorsey, was with us in the Noble band. At the time Pee Wee had a mania for playing high parts; he always asked me to give him stuff written way up on his horn. Sometimes I'd write things for him with the saxes playing underneath. There came a day when Pee Wee left and a trumpeter who couldn't hit those high notes replaced him. In desperation, we assigned the B-flat trumpet parts to Johnny Mince, now also with Tommy Dorsey, on B-flat clarinet and doubled the clarinet lead with Danny D'Andrea (a violinist who doubled on reeds) an octave lower on tenor sax. That's how the clarinet-lead sound, which people call "our style" started.'

Towards the end of the year, Ray Noble was offered a new contract. He was asked to join the Burns and Allen radio show which emanated from Hollywood. Ray had come to know the famous comedy team while filming *The Big Broadcast*, and George and Gracie had been impressed not only by Ray's musicianship; they had also fallen in love with his English accent. The idea that the bandleader could play an active part in a comedy show had been firmly established by George's best friend, Jack Benny, when he had cast Phil Harris as the hard-drinking Southern ignoramus in his own successful comedy series. Ray accepted the offer and thus embarked upon a whole new career as a radio personality.

Unfortunately, *The Burns And Allen Show* had already signed a featured singer, which meant that if Al stayed with the band, though he might be given an occasional song to sing, his role would inevitably remain a minor one.

Al showed Ray an offer he had received to do a variety tour in England. Ray advised him to take it. 'If it's successful and you don't want me any more,' said Ray, 'then the best of luck.' And that was the way they parted. In January 1937, Al and Marjie sailed for England on the SS *Berengaria*.

Nobody really knows why Al Bowlly left the United States so abruptly. Certainly the variety tour offer never materialized.

'It might have been that temper of his,' suggests Nat Gonella. It is rumoured in some quarters that he became involved with a gangster's girlfriend and was advised to leave New York in a hurry. Whatever the reason for his leaving, it is impossible to look upon Al's American adventure and see it as a success. Easier in fact, to see it as something of a tragedy. A tragedy of mis-timing.

In 1934, when Al had first arrived in America, band singers were still just another member of the orchestra. They weren't even paid as much as the regular sidemen, unless they were also instrumentalists for whom singing was just a second string to their bow. The only band vocalist who had successfully become a singing star was the old groaner himself, Bing Crosby, and he was unique.

By 1935, when Al was singing with Ray Noble at the plush and exclusive Rainbow Room, a full-scale revolution was being mounted elsewhere. In Hollywood, at the Palomar Ballroom, Benny Goodman was inaugurating the swing era, and by the summer of 1936 it would be well under way. In 1936 Artie Shaw, with his first big band, was playing at the Lexington Hotel; Tommy Dorsey was at the Hotel Lincoln and Goodman, already the 'King of Swing', was holding court nightly in the Manhattan Room of the Pennsylvania Hotel.

The status of the band singer began to change. To quote George Simon: 'How important were the vocalists to the big bands? Very! Some hipper jazz-oriented fans may have resented them and their intrusions. But in the overall picture, it was the singers who provided the most personal, the most literal and often the most communicative link between the bandstands and the dance floors, between stages and seats, and between recording and radio studios and the perennial "unseen audiences".'

In a *Metronome* poll taken in 1936, Al Bowlly was voted second in popularity only to Kenny Sargent, the singer with Glen Gray and the Casa Loma Orchestra; Crosby won third place.

By 1938, the big bands and their singers were dominating the entertainment scene. Among the top twenty bands of that year were Jimmy Dorsey with Bob Eberle; Benny Goodman with Martha Tilton; The Casa Loma Orchestra with Kenny Sargent;

Kay Kyser with Ginny Sims; Glenn Miller with Marion Hutton and Bob Eberle's brother, Ray; Artie Shaw with Billie Holiday; and Chick Webb with Ella Fitzgerald.

In February 1940, a skinny young singer named Frank Sinatra made his first records with Tommy Dorsey; in 1942, he decided to go solo and make a little showbiz history. The event which had pushed the band singers into such a commanding position had been the recording strike called by the national president of the American Federation of Musicians, James Caesar Petrillo. On 1 August, Petrillo ordered his musicians to stop all recordings until such time as the record companies would agree to pay a royalty on all recordings broadcast and played on juke boxes. Decca held out against him until September 1943, and a month later Capitol capitulated. But Columbia and Victor, who between them recorded most of the big-name bands, held out until November 1944. Over two years without a musician! George Simon tells the rest of the story: 'The strike couldn't have been more ill-timed. The girls at home and the boys overseas or in camps were equally lonely, equally sentimental, and for the most part preferred to listen to Frank Sinatra crooning instead of Harry James blaring, or to Peggy Lee whispering instead of Gene Krupa banging his drums. The time was ripe for the singers, with their personalized messages, and the strike helped them blossom by leaving the entire popular recording field wide open to them. It was theirs to take over, and take it over they did.'

By the war's end, the world of popular music had become primarily a singer's world, not only on records but also on the air. Radio shows which had once featured the top bands like Glenn Miller, Benny Goodman, Artie Shaw and the Dorseys, were now the exclusive domain of the singers: Frank Sinatra, Perry Como, Dick Haymes, Dinah Shore, Jo Stafford and Peggy Lee.

If only Al Bowlly had stayed on in America, what glittering prizes might he not have won? As it was, he came home to find his place usurped by other, younger singers. He had missed the boat both ways.

Welcome Home

On 16 January 1937, Al Bowlly landed at Southampton. He told reporters who met him: 'I am starting all over again, and I hope my singing and my band won't let down anybody who has a good opinion of me.'

Things had changed while he had been away. There was a new king, and that one-time regular patron of The Monseigneur —the Prince of Wales—had cancelled his membership and left the country. London's atmosphere had grown more sombre, and the dance bands, too, had lost some of their glamour. Don Barrigo recalls that Archer Street (the meeting-place for unemployed musicians) was filled more than ever with 'peanut-lunchers'! Musicians were now more likely to find themselves on the road, doing one-night stands in variety theatres, town halls, and palais, instead of enjoying the cosy dinner-jacketed luxury of the smart restaurants and hotels. However, there was still money to be made in the business, as Al's friend Nat Gonella had proved when he left Lew Stone's band in 1935 to go out on his own. Billed as 'Nat Gonella and his Georgians', he put on a well-produced variety act—a clever blend of hot jazz, romantic crooning and visual comedy that clicked with audiences all over the country, and set a new style for musical stage shows. Entertainment was the name of the game; audiences now *expected* a band to be a complete variety show in itself.

Al Bowlly set his sights on this same goal. His plan was to go on the road with a new seven-piece 'hot' combination, to be known as 'Al Bowlly and his Radio City Rhythm Makers'. From America, Al had already written to his brother Misch in Johannesburg, inviting him to join the band on piano. In London, he recruited Percy Hampton (drums), Derek Bailey (bass) and Archie Slavin (guitar). The front line brought together Don Barrigo (tenor sax, from Nat Gonella's Georgians), Teddy White (clarinet and baritone sax), Bert Green (trumpet) and Miff Ferrie (trombone). The tour was organized by impresario Leonard Urry, who had already set the wheels in motion while Al was in America. After seven weeks of rehearsal, the band made its début on 1 March 1937 at the Birmingham Empire. Before the curtain rose, the packed house heard the band strike up and then, from behind the dropped curtain, the unmistakable voice of Al Bowlly:

>Say, don't you remember?
>They called me Al.
>It was Al all the time.
>Say, don't you remember?
>I'm your pal!
>Buddy, can you spare a dime?

And they did remember, and showed their pleasure at his return, He sang 'Organ Grinder's Swing', 'The Very Thought of You', 'Marta', and finished with 'Tiger Rag'. *Melody Maker* duly reported: 'Al is singing better than ever; he is the logical reply to the anti-crooning brigade. His magnetic personality carries the whole show; his appealing voice pulls the heart strings and is meat for the rhythm fans too. His show is himself in all his moods, and London fans should not miss the show, which opens on Monday at the Paramount Theatre in Tottenham Court Road.'

After London, the Rhythm Makers were scheduled to embark on a thirteen-week provincial tour. Instead the band broke up after four weeks. What went wrong? According to Nat Gonella, Al found it difficult to re-adjust to English attitudes: 'In America they teach you to become big time. Even though you've made your name in England, once you've been to America and come back, you feel a bit more power. *You've* been to America, and these guys are all still here. I'm sure that Al thought he was going to be a sensation when he came back to England; instead, nobody wanted to know him. He didn't get big-headed in the sense of friendship—he'd still go and have a cup of tea with anyone who had known him. But you could see that his ego was hurt. He loved the applause and the success and all of that, so coming back here must have brought him down to earth.'

Certainly Al's inexperience as bandleader and producer played its part in the band's downfall. He didn't notice that his fellow-musicians were beginning to grumble about their roles in the show. They had not expected to find themselves as mere accompanists to a star singer. They were also unhappy about the way the tour was financed for, in business matters, Al was a babe-in-arms. 'He was taken for a ride left, right and centre,' says Tiny Winters. 'He was a very trusting bloke. Trusting and simple—not simple-minded, but rather simple and naive in his dealings with people. He wasn't cut out to be a leader. Really, he needed someone to look after him! He needed a good manager who understood him, and could organize his work for him, prepare his material, and produce his songs in the way they needed to be produced. Lew Stone did this for him, of course, in The Monseigneur days; and, in America, Ray Noble and Bill Harty looked after him. On his own, he was lost.'

There was another problem. His voice was going. He had been troubled with periodic sore throats since leaving America, and by the time the Rhythm Makers arrived in Dublin in early April he had lost his voice altogether, and could only conduct the band. A show built around a star can't survive without him: at the end of their week in Dublin, the demoralized Rhythm Makers disbanded and went their separate ways. Along with his voice, Al Bowlly lost most of his American savings, which he had invested in the tour.

The Rhythm Makers had made no records during their few weeks together. In fact, between his last New York recording session in October 1936 and a session for HMV in London in June 1937, Al Bowlly seems to have done no recording work at all, which certainly suggests that something was very seriously wrong. He later described, to a friend, his sensations on the day he woke up and found that his voice had gone: 'I stayed in bed. I cried and went on crying. I tried to force my voice—tried to force out some sound, to swear at myself, to give vent somehow. I reckon I knew how a woman would feel when she sees her child dying. The voice was gone—oh, but I can't begin to tell you how I felt. There aren't enough words.'

The source of the problem was soon diagnosed as a wart on Al's vocal chords. It seems that the only surgeon capable of performing the delicate and expensive operation which would save his voice was a top man working in New York. Al turned to his old friends for help, and found them wanting. Eventually his brother Misch raised some cash, and in the autumn of 1937 Bowlly returned to America for the operation. It is said that he had to sing during the operation, to guide the surgeon's knife! Whether that's true or not, the operation was certainly a success, to Al's very great relief. 'I've never been so happy, so cheerful, so contented of mind,' he said afterwards. 'I think right now I'm the happiest man in the world. I've got something that I've been looking for all my life. Honest to God, in my whole life—and I've had some good times.'

What exactly he had found isn't clear, but he certainly threw himself back into his work with renewed enthusiasm and vigour. In one session in New York, he recorded six titles for HMV, including 'I Can Dream, Can't I?', 'Sweet as a Song', and 'Outside of Paradise'. Then, in December, he sat sail again for England, determined to re-establish himself. *Melody Maker* heralded his return under the headline 'Al Bowlly's Dramatic Comeback', and reported his claim that he was now, miraculously, singing even better than before. Lew Stone's widow, Joyce, agrees: 'In some ways I think his voice was slightly more mellow after the operation. Even so, it wasn't easy for Al to get back. You see, while he'd been away, a lot of other singers had come to the fore: Alan Kane, Sam Browne and Jack Plant were very much in evidence. Women, too, were now being used more. I think Al had a problem. Lew would certainly have re-employed him, but Lew was doing stage shows for Jack Hulbert and Cecily Courtneidge, so he wasn't working at night. He did use Al on all his recording sessions and broadcasts.'

Other friends also rallied round and, in the first few months of 1938, Al made records with the orchestras of Ronnie Munro, Maurice Winnick, Sidney Lipton, Mantovani, Felix Mendelssohn, Reginald Williams, Oscar Rabin and Geraldo. His appetite for work was enormous, and he was clearly enjoying himself again. Peter Heron was a young singer at the time, and remembers his first meeting with Al: 'I was one of the Five Herons—a harmony group, consisting of myself, my brother Tony, and my three sisters Joan, Wendy and Kay. The group was well established on the stage, and on radio. We were approached, through an agent, by Al Bowlly, and asked if we would make a recording with him for HMV, as a backing group. We were hesitant at first, as this kind of arrangement of crooner with backing group had not been done before in Europe or America, and furthermore we had never heard of Al Bowlly. Later we learned that he had been in America for some years. But all our doubts were eliminated when we met Al. He was one of the most dynamic people we had ever met in the business.

'The preparation and rehearsing for the recording was spread over quite a long period, so we were able to get to know him rather well. He was so full of enthusiasm and energy that every session would leave us drained—but not him. To illustrate a point, he would often leap on the grand piano. He was quite a short man, but with powerful shoulders and very strong hands: as he always greeted you by shaking hands, it was jolly painful. Al told us he was forty-three years old, and he certainly did not look any more than that. We understood that he came from the Argentine.'

In the summer of 1938, Lew Stone invited Al to join his band for the gala opening of a new holiday camp at Clacton. Billy Butlin, who had saved for fifteen years before he could afford to buy a sixty-acre field at Skegness, had opened his first camp there in 1936. He offered all-in holidays for £4 a head, and the response was overwhelming. By 1938, when the government officially recognized the idea of paid holidays, the camps were spreading around the coastline. Billy Butlin really went to town for the Clacton opening, as Joyce Stone recalls:

> A lot of stars were booked to go down for a fortnight: Lew Stone's band with Al Bowlly, Mantovani and his Orchestra, Gracie Fields, Vic Oliver, Maskell and Pouson the tennis stars, Horace Lindrum and Joe Davis the snooker players. Since Al

was a very good snooker player, and Lew wasn't a bad snooker player, they played against Davis and Lindrum for the holiday-makers to watch.

During the day—I don't know why—all the musicians wore maroon jerseys with white stripes. This was for afternoon sessions, should it be wet. And of course they had to play in the ballroom at night: but I have a feeling that they even played in jerseys there. I don't think they wore dinner jackets. I don't think Butlins wanted that kind of rather formal atmosphere.

Al was certainly very popular, although I don't remember the crowds following him around then, as they used to do when he went on tour, before he went to America. He had a couple of girlfriends staying with him: the band brought their wives or girlfriends, and most of them stayed in the camp.

Marjie, Al's second wife, had left him soon after their return from America the year before. Nobody is quite clear exactly when, or how, it happened. For years she had been heroically tolerant of Al's philandering. A friend recalled a late-night conversation with Al and Marjie, in which they tried to picture themselves in old age, and Al had pleaded with Marjie: 'When I'm an old man, you will still let me have my little girlfriends, won't you?' Most people think Marjie left Al simply because her patience was exhausted. Some say she went back to New York, and became a hairdresser. When last heard of, she had re-married and was working in her husband's sweetshop in Boscombe, near Bournemouth.

One of Al's Butlins girlfriends, Helen, appears in a holiday snapshot taken there. Bandleader and sax player Chappie d'Amato remembers her, because she later married his sister's ex-husband. He describes her as a tall redhead. 'She was one of the Kensington girls who wanted to get to know musicians. Some of them went so far as to hang around in Portsmouth, in the hopes of meeting young American musicians off the transatlantic liners. They were desperate to get married so that they could go to the States.'

Al and Helen returned to London together after the Butlins stint. They found a flat in Piccadilly, in a block called Duke's Court, which was on the corner of Duke Street and Jermyn

Street. Chappie d'Amato visited them there, and got the impression that it was more like furnished rooms. There were very few possessions: 'It didn't seem like a home.'

In August Al joined Lew Stone for two more recording sessions, which included a duet à la Flanagan and Allen with a then relatively unknown young singer called Sid Colin. The title was 'Down and Out Blues'. Al also buried the hatchet with Don Barrigo, and recorded a version of 'Stardust' with Don Barrigo and his Hawaiian Swing. He did some broadcasting on BBC Radio's *Crooners Corner* and *Friends to Tea*. Monia Liter, who had taken a flat in the same block in Piccadilly, invited Al to take part in his Radio Luxembourg programme of *Music in the New Manner*. Sponsored by Black Magic chocolates, it was broadcast on Sunday afternoons, and Al was introduced as 'your singer of romantic songs'. He could also be heard in the Hinds Honey and Almond Cream programme on Radio Lyons: 'I Kiss Your Hand, Madame' was the signature tune.

In September, he waited anxiously—as the whole country did —to hear the outcome of Mr Chamberlain's momentous visits to Germany, and shared the general euphoria at the signing of the Anglo-German agreement with its built-in promise of 'peace in our time'. As a gentle reminder to Herr Hitler, Al recorded 'Never Break a Promise', with Geraldo and his orchestra.

In December, he was the guest of honour at the opening of the Scunthorpe *Palais de Danse* (a converted store in the High Street). The local paper reported: 'Despite a number of other dances in the town—all well supported—two hundred and fifty people attended the opening. Judged by London standards, the hall is not large, but it is cosy and has a very pleasant atmosphere. Friday's crowd filled it comfortably. It is furnished and decorated throughout in a tasteful colour scheme of brown, with lighting effects which lend real charm to the ballroom, which occupies the first floor. A comfortable café-lounge is housed on the ground floor. Al Bowlly sang seven numbers and had a terrific and well-deserved reception.' Even so, the picture conjured up by that report doesn't really compare with the kind of extraordinary scenes that had greeted Al Bowlly in 1932: for instance, at York, where the dancing stopped and more than 5,000 people packed the hall to hear their favourite radio star in person. There the queue for autographs had stretched all the way round the ballroom floor. Times had changed, and in 1938 new trends in popular music were emerging. In the heady, carefree post-Munich days, people wanted to *sing*. The elegant, polished, white-tie music of the dance bands didn't fit the national mood. In its place, on the crest of a wave of patriotic nostalgia, a song called 'The Lambeth Walk' suddenly became *the* hit song of 1938. Written by Noël Gay for the musical *Me and My Girl*, it was sung by Lupino Lane with appropriate movements—a kind of rolling cockney swagger, with over-the-shoulder thumbing, and occasional shouts of 'Oi!'. Soon everyone was doing it, and it became a dance craze in the palais. Hard on its heels came 'Hands, Knees and Boomps-a-daisy' (words and music by Annette Mills), which was equally popular.

1939 saw Al Bowlly back in London, still doing occasional recording dates with Geraldo, and still making personal appearances. But he was no longer making much impact with his audiences, and according to several reports he even suffered the ignominy of being booed off the stage by the dancers at Poplar Town Hall. Sidney Brown was the Entertainments Manager there and he recalls that:

> Al Bowlly did appear at the Assembly Hall in Poplar Town Hall, and there was some kind of bother. You see it was customary, in those days, to boost attendances for the dances by booking star radio singers to do a fifteen-minute 'spot' during a break in the dancing. But in those days, as in the present times, moronic youngsters were no respecters of persons, and several of the singers I booked received scant attention. This was no reflection on the performers; it was a case of casting pearls before swine, and I am sure that this was the situation in the case of Al Bowlly, because he was extremely popular with the dedicated fans. In short, to appear at a public dance was not, as they say today, his 'scene'.

So why did he do it? It seems an inescapable fact that, by now, Al was unable to pick and choose his bookings, as he had done in his heyday. He went where the work was, and took what was offered.

And now, when his fortunes were at perhaps their lowest ebb since his busking days ten years before, his voice gave out on him again. Was this coincidence, or does it suggest a psychosomatic reaction to his troubles? According to Monia Liter, his voice acted like a barometer gauging his well-being: 'When he first came back from America, he seemed to me to be very depressed. And when he did any work, his unhappiness showed in his work, because he was such an expressive singer.' Joe Crossman agrees: 'He put everything into his songs. He was a very sentimental person.' And Ray Noble: 'Al was a very simple man in many ways, and when he sang a love lyric it really got him. The sincerity came through. I have seen him sing at the mike in front of the band, and there've been tears in his eyes as he turned away after finishing. He was totally genuine.'

A record made in June 1939 with Bram Martin and his band featured a very lacklustre performance from Al of 'The Waves Of The Ocean Are Whispering Tonight'. After that, another severe throat infection prevented him from doing any singing at all, and he didn't enter a recording studio again until October. By that time, the outbreak of war had occasioned the closing down of all places of entertainment 'until the scale of attack is judged'. In a letter to *The Times*, George Bernard Shaw complained of this 'master-stroke of imaginative stupidity'. He suggested that 'all actors, variety artists, musicians and entertainers of all sorts should be exempted from every form of service except their own all-important professional one.' In fact, there was no great urgency for crooners and musicians to enlist: 'Wait till we send for you' was the order of their day. Men in their early twenties were not immediately required, and for those in their forties it looked like an even longer wait. Al was now forty-nine.

In December, he recorded 'Bella Bambina' and 'Somewhere In France With You' at HMV's studios. By then the closedown of theatres, cinemas and nightclubs had been lifted and the West End was once again open for business. Even so, Al, as a freelance singer, was not getting the work, so in January 1940, in a desperate attempt to make another fresh start, he formed a partnership with a singer called Jimmy Mesene. They called themselves 'The Radio Stars with Two Guitars', and they made their debut at the Theatre Royal, Newcastle. Mesene was a Maltese hunchback, son of a millionaire ship-owner. A BSc of Taunton University, and fluent in seven languages, he had entered the music business for fun. He was a real character, according to Nat Gonella: 'Like Al, he was a very excitable fellow. He used to sing with my band, and I remember him drinking a bottle of whisky in the dressing-room before going on stage. Then he'd forget the words of his song, and have to finish it in scat—ba de de dee da ba da da! But you had to get on with Jimmy Mesene, he was a very funny guy—he'd kiss you every moment if he could. Al and Jimmy made a good pair. I could imagine them in the wrestling ring together—that would have been good!'

1940 was not a good year to launch a new act. Although vocal groups like the Andrews Sisters and the Mills Brothers were beginning to rival the solo singers, neither Al nor Jimmy Mesene was a smart enough operator to get their act booked into the number one theatres. But they managed to put together a short provincial tour of lesser variety theatres, NAAFI canteens and palais.

In *Melody Maker*'s poll of readers' favourite vocalists, published in March 1940, Al Bowlly still made a reasonable showing, coming fourth. But Jimmy Mesene's name didn't even appear in the top twenty. Denny Dennis, Ambrose's featured vocalist, topped the poll. The other prominent names on the list were all singers who had a regular association with the leading bands: Chick Henderson (Joe Loss), Sam Browne (Jack Hylton), Sam Costa (Maurice Winnick), and Monte Rey (Geraldo). The favourite lady singer, by a mile, was Vera Lynn.

The two 'Radio Stars' staggered on through 1940. Al did some solo work on the side: occasional broadcasts with Lew Stone, recordings with Macari and his orchestra and Maurice Winnick. He got together with coloured bandleader Ken 'Snakehips' Johnson to record jazz arrangements of two Shakespeare sonnets —*Blow, Thou Winter Wind* and *It Was a Lover and His Lass*. Additional vocals on these sides were provided by The Henderson Twins (Dickie Henderson's sisters). Al was also invited to take part in a Sunday afternoon Jazz Jamboree at the Gaumont State Cinema, Kilburn, in aid of the Musicians' Benevolent Fund. It was quite a get-together and almost every big-name band in town was represented: Ambrose, Geraldo, Jack Harris, Ken 'Snakehips' Johnson, George Melachrino, Sid Phillips, Oscar Rabin, Sydney Torch. A number of musicians were embarrassed to find themselves booked to play with more than one band through irregular 'moonlighting' associations, which needed some explaining away! The jamboree raised more than £4,000 and, for Al Bowlly, it must have been an occasion of great nostalgia, re-uniting him with many old friends from the Roy Fox and Lew Stone bands: Joe Crossman, Tiny Winters, Ivor Mairants, Alfie Noakes, Don Barrigo, Harry Gold, Sid Buckman, Bill Shakespeare, Jock Jacobson, and 'Poggy' Pogson. A notable absentee was Nat Gonella, who had already been drafted into the Pioneer Corps, and was en route to Africa.

The Jazz Jamboree was really the last, mighty blast of the 'Golden Age' of dance bands. Over the next few months, as the phoney war became all too real, the dance bands were decimated by the call-up. By the autumn, the German *blitzkrieg* was beginning to dislodge the few surviving stalwarts from the West End.

A Charmed Life

The raids usually began at dusk. Shops and offices closed at 4 pm. When the siren was heard, people collected their ration books, identity cards and other important documents, plus gas masks, blankets, and food. They would hurry to the nearest communal shelter—to their own or their neighbour's sandbagged basement, or to the Anderson shelter in the garden. The early raids featured high-explosive bombs weighing up to five hundred pounds, plus occasional incendiaries. The largest bombs came silently by parachute, including the eight-foot-long land-mines which caused enormous devastation. During October and November 1940, some 18,000 bombs were dropped on London alone.

Al was still living with Helen in the Jermyn Street flat. One of his neighbours there was Anona Winn, with whom he had sung a number of duets in broadcasts before the war. Monia Liter and Beatrice Lillie and her mother also had flats there. During the worst raids they would all meet in the cellar, but Anona Winn recalls that, even in the early days of the Blitz, Al occasionally refused to come down to the shelter. 'It became a sort of standing joke that when we were checking up to see where everybody was, he would still be upstairs in bed.' According to Joe Crossman, Al's bravado stemmed from a strange experience he had had. 'In one of the first daylight raids, he happened to be walking in Brewer Street when a bomb fell right in the middle of the street. When it exploded, the force of the blast seemed to go in one direction—*away* from Al—and he was unharmed. And from then on, he really thought he had a charmed life, which is why he often ignored the air-raid warnings.'

As London began to accustom itself to the bombings, people became more blasé about taking shelter. The communal shelters were cramped and stuffy. Some restaurants, particularly those below ground level, were considered to be impregnable: indeed, the Café de Paris, in Coventry Street near Piccadilly, used to be advertised as 'London's safest restaurant'. Yet on 8 March 1941, at about 9.45 pm, two hundred-pound bombs fell into the Café de Paris. One exploded in front of the bandstand, at approximately chest-height among the dancers, killing the bandleader, Ken 'Snakehips' Johnson, tenor-sax player Dave Williams, and thirty-two patrons, and seriously wounding sixty more. The other bomb didn't explode, but burst on impact with the dance floor, scattering its stinking yellow contents over the dead and dying, and making a small hole in the parquet floor. Leslie Hutchinson, the trumpeter and a good friend of Ken Johnson, was unhurt, though shocked: 'I grabbed my trumpet and off I went. A fellow showed me the way out. Everybody seemed to be asking "What's happening, what's happened down there?" I said, "Oh, I don't know man, I just come up." I was covered with dust. A man came up to me and said "Have you heard anything about Mr Johnson?" I said "No, I haven't heard anything." He was followed by a lady who said "You haven't seen Mr Johnson?", and I said: "No, I haven't seen him." She said "Oh well, you'll hear, you'll hear." And then I was told the news, that Ken wasn't with us anymore. Afterwards I went to a nightclub, got my trumpet out of the case and had a blow, just to sober things up a bit. I know some people may think it wasn't the thing to do, but what else could I do in the circumstances? I thought it was the best thing to do. I had a blow, followed by a long walk home.'

Al Bowlly was shocked (as indeed was the whole of the music profession) at the death of 'Snakehips'. It is said that the event had added significance for Al because earlier that same day he had received a letter from a friend telling him of a dream she'd had in which Al was talking to a coloured man, when suddenly both of them were blown to pieces. True or false, the story is now part of Bowlly 'lore', and it may be one of the reasons why he is widely believed to have been killed in the Café de Paris. In fact he outlived his friend 'Snakehips' by five weeks.

On 2 April he recorded, with Jimmy Mesene, an Irving Berlin song about Hitler called 'When That Man is Dead and Gone':

> ... we'll go dancing down the street,
> Kissing everyone we meet.
> When that man is dead and gone,
> What a day to wake up on
> What a way to greet the dawn.
> Some fine day the news will flash
> Satan with a small mustache is asleep beneath the lawn.
> When that man is dead and gone.

It's an awful record, and should never have been released. Both singers are out of tune, their phrasing and timing rarely coincide, and the guitar playing is erratic. For the other side, they recorded 'Nicky the Greek Has Gone'.

The duo then played a number of engagements in the West Country, and broadcast from the BBC's wartime variety base at Bristol. On Monday, 14 April, they started a week's engagement at the Rex Theatre, High Wycombe. John Watsham was the proprietor at the time: 'I was running ciné-variety that week, and my top-of-the-bill was "Al Bowlly and Jimmy Mesene—the Anglo-Greek Ambassadors of Song—Two Voices and Guitars in Harmony". The week got off to a bad start as I had engaged a new organist who, although perfectly adequate for his solo spot, turned out to have had absolutely no experience in accompanying. In the middle of their act at the first house, Al, who had been stamping out the beat as hard as he could to "Buddy, Can You Spare a Dime?" stopped, advanced to the organist, raised his guitar menacingly, and told him he was killing the act and that if he played another note he would kill him. Between the two houses, the organist met with a mysterious accident, and never appeared again, though he did sue me and, I am happy to say, lost the day. On the Tuesday, we scouted round and found a local church organist who proved to be more than adequate, and agreed to fill in for the rest of the week. Little did we guess what that week would have in store for us! After the second house on the Wednesday night, 16 April, we were having a little private party in a nearby hostelry—Al, Jimmy, my manager Captain Talbot Bullock, my wife and myself. The night wore on, and it was a good party, Al being about the only stone-cold sober one. I believe he was always a teetotaller, and I can still recall my horror at the amount of tomato juice he managed to consume. He suddenly told us he was leaving to catch the last train to London. He was adamant, despite all our efforts to make him change his mind. Even cutting off his tie was to no avail and he just disappeared into the night leaving us to continue without him. Little did we realize then that we should never see him again.'

Al arrived in London in time to fill a late-night solo spot at the Berkeley Hotel, where he met up with a friend, a BBC engineer. In the early hours of the morning, they went back to Al's flat for a meal. When his friend had gone, Al went to bed with a cowboy book. That night, the Luftwaffe launched its heaviest raid on London. The German High Command issued a communiqué: 'As a reprisal for the destruction caused by the British Air Force to historical buildings and monuments in Berlin last Wednesday, several hundred bombers tonight attacked London in successive waves for ten hours.'

In the West End, three theatres, three cinemas, four large hotels, eight hospitals, two famous stores and hundreds of homes were hit by high explosives or incendiaries. Five of the raiders were brought down. One bomber crashed in flames into Campden Hill Road, with the pilot dead at the controls; later the bodies of two airmen who had baled out were discovered in Kensington High Street, badly mutilated.

In Jermyn Street, a landmine fell and exploded. It blew in all the windows of the Duke's Court flats, but, apparently, caused no major structural damage. As soon as the 'all clear' sounded, the porter went round all the flats to check that his tenants were unharmed. He found Al Bowlly dead on the floor beside his bed. He was unmarked, but the blast had killed him outright.

Where was Helen? According to Chappie d'Amato, she had gone out to buy cigarettes and so had escaped the explosion. That seems an eccentric thing to do at the height of the most intensive air-raid of the war. It's more likely that she was in the shelter, although that night her friends were not there to keep her company. Anona Winn was in Southampton, Monia Liter was in Bangor: 'I had gone there for a concert with Sandy MacPherson. When I got back to Jermyn Street on the morning after the raid, Bea Lillie met me in the hall. She said "We've had a terrible night—look here", and showed me a number of large sacks in the hall with labels on them. "These are the people who were killed last night." I saw that one of the sacks had Al Bowlly's name on the label. It was a terrible shock.'

The following day, the *Daily Mirror* announced: 'Other deaths in Wednesday night's raid were those of Lord Auckland, pilot and animal trainer, and Al Bowlly, crooner'. The *Sketch* reported: 'Lord and Lady Stamp dead ... killed during Wednesday night's raid. Lord Auckland and Al Bowlly, the well-known coloured singer, were also victims.' *Melody Maker* carried a full-page obituary, under the heading: 'Say, don't you remember, they called me Al ... ' Stanley Nelson wrote: 'these lines might well be the epitaph of one of the finest singers British jazz has ever known, and whenever they are heard in the future, they will always recall a lithe, muscular, bright-eyed figure "selling" his songs in a way that has never been excelled and rarely equalled by a Britisher.'

Jimmy Mesene rang John Watsham at High Wycombe to break the sad news. Watsham 'agreed that this was one occasion when the show just could not go on. Jimmy, however, said that he wanted to open again on the Friday, and spent the time building up a new act, "A Tribute to Al Bowlly". This of course included "Buddy, Can You Spare a Dime?", and Jimmy finished the week's booking with it.'

On Saturday 26 April, Al was buried in a communal grave of the Westminster Council Cemetery, Uxbridge Road, Hanwell. A minister of the Greek Orthodox Church conducted the funeral service; among the handful of friends who were present were Helen, Jimmy Mesene, and Chick Henderson. *Melody Maker* commented on the poor attendance, and announced that 'Arrangements are going forward to hold a service at the Greek Church in Bayswater, when all those who found it impossible to be at Hanwell will have the opportunity to pay their last respects to the grand singer and all-round good fellow who was Al Bowlly.' But, according to Joyce Stone, 'At the time of Al's death, so many people were being killed nightly in the blitz that, while naturally we were upset and sad, it had become almost a daily occurrence to lose a friend or someone in the profession whom you knew. And so one took it in one's stride. And one simply couldn't go to the funerals of all one's acquaintances and friends—life had to go on. There just wasn't time; and anyway it was very difficult to get to these places—one had no petrol. And if you were kept up half the night by air raids, you weren't in any fit state the next morning to go to somebody's funeral. So very few people went to Al's memorial service.'

Some days later, Lew Stone received a phone call from Helen. She'd found a new flat in the Edgware Road, and suggested that Lew might like to come round, and look through Al's possessions with her, to decide what should be done with them. When he got there, he was amazed to discover how little there was. No souvenirs or mementoes of his travels, no letters from friends or fans, no papers, contracts, clippings, prizes, lucky charms or treasured objects, no furniture or household goods of any kind. To the end, Al Bowlly travelled light. As a personal souvenir, Lew Stone took away six records, on the Decca label, featuring 'Lew Stone and his Monseigneur Band, with Vocal Refrain by Al Bowlly'.

AL BOWLLY DISCOGRAPHY
By Brian Rust and Clifford Harvey

Our purpose here is to list all the records known to have been made by Al Bowlly, who must be regarded as one of the greatest entertainers appearing before the public in the decade or so before the outbreak of World War II. There may be other records of which we have no sort of knowledge, and if any reader can come forward with documentary evidence of these in the form of the records themselves, we will be extremely grateful. We can at least say that in compiling the discography we have been able to hear all the issued titles, and even some of the rejects, made in England. Thanks to Mr Horst H. Lange, that redoubtable German discographer, we were allowed to hear several of the German recordings that were the first Al Bowlly solos as a vocalist, and which are now extremely rare. (His earlier sides, made in Calcutta in 1926 as banjo-guitarist with the Lequime Orchestra, are believed to be entirely non-vocal.)

The reader will observe that we have listed only the numbers of the original 78 rpm issues, although we are of course well aware that several long-playing and extended-play records have been issued in various parts of the world (notably the UK, USA and Australia). Reference to the current catalogues will show details of these, and their very existence indicates a widespread interest in the work of Al Bowlly.

During his earlier years in England, Al Bowlly made many records as the anonymous vocalist with many dance bands, of which a considerable number were studio groups arranged by the musical directors of companies no longer in existence. Determining their chronological place was not easy, but we believe it to be accurate to a month, basing our statements on the release dates of each record, obtained from the files of *The Gramophone*. In the case of some of the Edison Bell records, we are indebted to Mr Patrick Saul, Secretary of the British Institute of Recorded Sound, in whose library exist some test pressings bearing exact recording dates, and who allowed us to examine them aurally and visually.

At this point, we feel we must also offer our special thanks to Mr Geoff Milne, who is not only a keen collector of Bowlly records himself, but is also in a position to allow us to see and hear evidence of the existence of all Al Bowlly's work for Decca Records, and thus establish beyond any doubt his presence on them, together with the dates on which they were made.

Our gratitude is also due to the American collectors, Mr Harry Avery, of California, whose Ray Noble discography was published in the now-obsolete magazine *Record Changer* in June 1951, and Mr William W. Gilbert of New York, while Mr Jacob Schneider of New York provided copies in perfect condition of the majority of Al Bowlly's American recordings. Details of the sides made in 1935, 1936 and 1937 for RCA Victor were provided by Mr Brad McCuen in the RCA Victor office in New York, and Miss Agnes Leach and Mrs G. Platford of EMI, Ltd, Hayes, Middlesex. Mr George Port supplied exact information on English recordings for EMI, and all the Australian issue numbers came from three truly indefatigable collectors there, Messrs Peter Burgis, Jack Forehan and Mike Sutcliffe.

It is only comparatively recently that many of Al Bowlly's most obscure records have come to light, and that they have done so is due for the most part to our own insistence on buying and listening to an incalculable number of the most worthless records of the Bowlly era, our reward every once in a while being the discovery of a hitherto unsuspected 'find'. In this, we have had the assistance of Mr Ivor Holland, not himself a Bowlly collector, but in sympathy with our aim of building a complete collection of records as a suitable memorial and tribute to the man who made them.

As with records by almost every reputable artist who becomes the object of attention by collectors, so with Al Bowlly there are rumoured recordings of his work that have not, and in some cases, cannot be substantiated. For some time, the record on Brunswick of 'Siboney' by the Anglo-Persians was regarded as a Bowlly item. A moment's consideration of the facts (it was recorded in New York in 1930) will serve to illustrate the stupidity of this contention. The very rare item by the Odonians on the garish flexible Trusound label, 'If I Could Paint Your Picture On The Moon', has turned out to be by one of Bowlly's less successful imitators, and though proof is still lacking, we feel that it was Billy Scott-Coomber who sang on Percy Chandler's Piccadilly record of 'Darling, I'm Longing To Greet You' (he is undoubtedly present on 'Good Friends' on the reverse). Billy Cotton's two Metropole sides, 'Where Have You Been All My Life?' and 'I Don't Know Why I Do It', which was once attributed to Al Bowlly, are known to have been sung by the leader himself, and the elusive Edison Bell Winner 5560 of 'No More Love', for long attributed to Bowlly on no known grounds, has been discovered and found to be by Sam Browne, issued thus on Panachord also.

In this discography, we have listed all the known records on which Al Bowlly's voice can be heard, or on which we are nine-tenths certain he can be heard. Where other voices are audible, we have attempted to identify them, and have included the names in parentheses after the title.

When Al Bowlly is heard as the incidental vocalist with a dance band or instrumental group, the paragraph listing such records is headed 'with such-and-such' (if his name is shown on the label, the record number is followed by an asterisk *); when he is the principal artist, the supporting group is shown in the heading as 'Acc. by so-and-so'. Identification of each member of an individual band or group has not been attempted, as we feel that this is not generally of much interest to those who collect Al Bowlly's records for his presence on them. Nor have we listed LP or EP catalogue numbers; for these, may we refer our readers to the current catalogues of the major labels?

The following abbreviations of record labels are used (makes not included in this list are given in full in the Discography):

BB—Bluebird (American)
Bcst—Broadcast (2500 series 'Broadcast Twelve Dance' (Orange label); 3000 series 'Broadcast Super Twelve' (Red label); 600 series 8-inch red label with white insert and black lettering.
Br—Brunswick
Cel—Celebrity
Col—Columbia
Dec—Decca (no-prefix—American; F-, K-, M- —British)
Dmn—Dominion
EBR—Edison Bell Radio (8-inch)
EBW—Edison Bell Winner
El—Electrola (German)
Film—Filmophone
Gr—Deutsche Grammophon (German)
HMV—His Master's Voice (all British except EA (Australian), N (Indian) and no prefix (Canadian).
Hom—Homochord (German)
Imp—Imperial
May—Mayfair   Met—Metropole
Oct—Octocros
Pana—Panachord
Par—Parlophone
Pic—Piccadilly
Pol—Polydor (German; export label for Deutsche Grammophon); W series Australian
Re—Regal (all British except G-20000 series (Australian))
Vic—Victor (American)

All the above labels are of British manufacture unless otherwise stated.

With ARTHUR BRIGGS'S SAVOY SYNCOPATORS' ORCHESTRA
Berlin, c July 1927

592bd; B-41819	Song Of The Wanderer	Gr/Pol 21034*
593bd; B-41821	Muddy Water	Gr/Pol 21035*
599bd; B-41820	Hallelujah	Gr/Pol 21034*
600bd; B-41823	Miss Annabelle Lee	Gr/Pol 21036*
601bd; B-41824	Memphis	–
602bd; B-41825	Rio Rita	Gr/Pol 21037

603bd; B-41822   I'm Looking For A Girl Named   Gr/Pol 21035*
                    Mary
604bd; B-41826   Cheritza   Gr/Pol 21037

   NOTE: Al Bowlly's presence on 601, 602 and 604 has not been confirmed, but it seems very likely he did make them.

Acc. by own uke., Edgar Adeler (pno.)   Berlin, September 11, 1927.
M-19372   Blue Skies   Hom 4-2386
M-19373   Say, Mister! Have You Met Rosie's Sister   —

With FRED BIRD, THE SALON SYMPHONIC JAZZ BAND.
                                        Berlin, September 12, 1927.
M-19381-2   Ain't She Sweet?   Hom 4-2389
M-19382   In A Little Spanish Town   —

Acc. by own gtr.-1, bjo.-2, Fred Bird (vln.), Edgar Adeler (pno.)
                                        Berlin, September 23, 1927.
M-19444   I'm Alone In Athlone-2   Hom 4-2418
M-19445   Because I Love You-1   —

The next four titles probably belong to this period; the acc. is unknown.
            A Dream Of You   Hom 4-2411
            Muddy Water   —
            All Day Long   Hom 4-2414
            I'm Looking For A Bluebird (To Chase   —
               My Blues Away)

With GEORGE CARHART'S NEW YORKERS JAZZ ORCHESTRA.
                                        Berlin, September 28, 1927
M-19451   Sunny Disposish   Hom 4-2420

Acc. by own gtr.-1, own steel gtr.-3, or own uke.-4, with Heinz Lewy (pno.)
                                        Berlin, November 18, 1927.
M-19566   When You Played The Organ And I   Hom 4-2459
            Sang 'The Rosary'-3
M-19569   Dear Little Gadabout-4   —
            Ev'ry Little Thing I Do   Hom 4-2460
            Rosy Cheeks-1   —
            My Regular Girl-1   Hom 4-2461
            Positively—Absolutely   —

With ARTHUR BRIGGS'S SAVOY SYNCHOPATORS' ORCHESTRA.
                                        Berlin, c December 1927
681bd; B-41887   Ain't She Sweet?   Gr/Pol 21124*
682bd; B-41883   Do The Black Bottom With Me   Gr/Pol 21122*
684bd; B-41884   Souvenirs   —   * W-104
691bd; B-41889   Since I Found You   Gr/Pol 21125
693bd; B-41895   Who-oo? You-oo, That's Who!   Gr/Pol 21128*
694bd; B-41893   Rosy Cheeks   Gr/Pol 21127*
695bd; B-41896   Roses For Remembrance   Gr/Pol 21128*

700bd; B-41886	Why Don't You?	Gr/Pol 21123
701bd; B-41890	I'm Coming, Virginia	Gr/Pol 21125*
702bd; B-41888	It All Depands On You	Gr/Pol 21124*
703bd; B-41892	Oole-De-Doo	Gr/Pol 21126

With FRED BIRD, THE SALON SYMPHONIC JAZZ BAND

Berlin, c January 1928

	Rio Rita	Hom 4-2496
	Souvenirs	–

With ARTHUR BRIGGS'S SAVOY SYNCOPATORS' ORCHESTRA.

Berlin, c January 1928.

717bd; B-41897	Dreamy Amazon	Gr/Pol 21129
718bd; B-41899	Me And My Shadow	Gr-Pol 21130*
719bd; B-41900	Are You Happy?	– *
720bd; B-41898	You Should See My Tootsie	Gr/Pol 21129
721bd?	My Regular Girl	Gr/Pol 21131
722bd; B-41903	Maybe I Will	Gr/Pol 21132
723bd?	I'm Walking On Air	Gr/Pol 21131
734bd; B-41894	Sometimes I'm Happy	Gr/Pol 21127* W-103
737bd; B-41904	Baby Your Mother	Gr/Pol 21132
740bd;	Take Your Finger Out Of Your Mouth	Gr/Pol 21134
741bd; B-41906	Vo-Do-Do-De-O Blues	Gr/Pol 21133
	Sweet Marie	Gr/Pol 21134
	The Little White House	Gr/Pol 21135, W-102, W-104
	Ain't That A Grand And Glorious Feeling?	– –

NOTE: Al Bowlly's presence on the following Arthur Briggs sides is still unconfirmed: 691, 700, 703, 717, 720, 722, 723, 737, 740, 741. On matrices 683, 685, 686, 692 and 738 there is apparently no vocal work at all.

With JOHN ABRIANI'S SIX or JOHN ABRIANI AND HIS ORCHESTRA (on M-19833).

Berlin, January 17, 1928.

M-19826	I Love No-One But You	Hom 4-2514
M-19827	My Blue Heaven	Hom 4-2511, 4-2611
M-19828	Just Once Again	Hom 4-2512, 4-2613

Berlin, January 18, 1928.

M-19829	A Shady Tree	Hom 4-2613
M-19830	Are You Thinking Of Me Tonight?	Hom 4-2612
M-19831	My Regular Girl	Hom 4-2512, 4-2611
M-19832	Shaking The Blues Away	Hom 4-2514

NOTE: Matrix M-19832 and M-19834 were never issued; M-19835 has no vocal.

          Berlin, January 20, 1928.
M–19840 All I Want Is You   Hom 4–2532
M–19841 Can't You Hear Me Say 'I Love You'? –

With FRED ELIZALDE AND HIS MUSIC. London, c July 25, 1928.
   Just Imagine   Br 189
   Wherever You Are   –
   After My Laughter Came Tears Rejected

With VAN PHILLIPS AND HIS BAND. London, November 12, 1928.
A–8089–1 Sometimes   Col 5209

With FRED ELIZALDE AND HIS MUSIC. London, c November 21, 1928.
BB–146–1 If I had You   Br 3948*
            London, December 1928.
BB–170–3 Misery Farm   Br 206
BB–171–1 I'm Sorry, Sally   –

With PERCIVAL MACKEY AND HIS CONCERT ORCHESTRA.
            London, April 1929.
 1782 When The Lilac Blooms Again Pic 288
 1783–2 Up In The Clouds   Pic 264, Met 1141,
              Oct 291
 Note: Piccadilly 264 as THE EVER-BRIGHT BOYS.

With LINN MILFORD AND HIS HAWAIIAN PLAYERS AND/OR SINGERS. ('Linn Milford' is Len Fillis, the South African-born guitarist and banjoist).
            London, May 15, 1929.
A–9019–1 Honeymoon Chimes   Re G–9362, G–20550
 NOTE: Other titles from this session have no vocal refrains.
            London, November 5, 1929.
A–9714–1 Lay My Head Beneath A Rose Re G–9442, G–20654
A–9717–1 Last Night I Dreamed You Kissed Me – –
 NOTE: Other titles from this session have no vocal refrains.

With THE HONOLULU SERENADERS (same group as last).
            London, c November, 1929.
 1577–2 The Pagan Love Song (with Les Allen) Dmn A–219
 1578–1 This Is Heaven (with Les Allen) Dmn A–242
 1579–1 S'posin' (with Les Allen) –
 NOTE: Matrix 1580, the reverse of 1577, has a vocal by Les Allen only.

With FRED ELIZALDE'S RHYTHMICIANS, directed by ADRIAN ROLLINI.
            London, December 4, 1929.
 3262 After The Sun Kissed The World Met 1241, Oct 367
    Goodbye
 3263 If Anything Happened To You – –

With LINN MILFORD AND HIS HAWAIIAN SINGERS.
            London, January 24, 1930
A–9994–1 An Old Italian Love Song Re MR–28

A-9995-1, -2	Love Made A Gypsy Out Of Me	Rejected
A-9996-1, -2	Waiting At The End of The Road	–
A-9997-1	In The Moonlight	Re MR-28

With JAY WILBUR AND HIS BAND. This item is not certainly by Al Bowlly; it has a vocal duet between Cavan O'Connor and another voice that sounds very much like Bowlly's. No other titles from this session have so far been found.

London, c February 1930.

1634-2	Rio Rita	Dmn A-246

With LINN MILFORD AND HIS HAWAIIAN PLAYERS.

London, March 7, 1930.

WAR-36-1	Gypsy Dream Rose	Rejected
WAR-37-1	Silvery Moon	Re MR-79, G-21246

With THE BROOKLYN BROADCASTERS (Dominion C-303), HONOLULU SERENADERS (Dominion C-319), HAWAIIAN OCTET (Celebrity 4390); apparently a Len Fillis group. London, c March 1930.

1717-1	Silv'ry Moon	Dmn C-319, Cel 4390
1718-2	Happy Days Are Here Again	Dmn C-303
1721-1	Gypsy Dream Rose	Dmn C-319, Cel 4390

NOTE: Matrices 1719 and 1720 have not yet been traced.

With EDGAR ADELER'S HAWAIIAN PLAYERS, London, c March 1930.

S-759-1	Silv'ry Moon	Sterno 406
S-760	Land Of The Might-Have-Been	Sterno 594
S-761	Somehow	Sterno 429
S-763-1	Lazy Lou'siana Moon	Sterno 406

NOTE: Matrix S-762 has no vocal refrain.

Acc. by Gideon Fagan (pno.) Hayes, Middlesex, June 10, 1930.

Bb-19460-1	Ou Kaapstad is mij Hemel-Land	Rejected
Bb-19461-3	Sy's in die Pad (both in Afrikaans)	HMV FJ-133*

Acc. by small orchestra, directed by Ray Noble.

Hayes, Middlesex, June 30, 1930.

Bb-19493-2	Alleenig (in Afrikaans)	HMV FJ-100
Bb-19494-1, -2, -3	Sy's mij klein Liefie (in Afrikaans)	Rejected?
Bb-19495-1	Sunshire	Rejected

With LINN MILFORD AND HIS HAWAIIAN SINGERS.

London, July 2, 1930.

WAR-234-1	Every Little Kindness (Makes An Angel Smile)	Re MR-197, G-20979
WAR-235-2	My Angel Mother	Re MR-128, G-20825
WAR-236-2	The Golden Gates Of Paradise	– –
WAR-237-1	The Hymns My Mother Used to Sing	Re MR-197, G-20979

Acc. by small orchestra, directed by Ray Noble.

Hayes, Middlesex, July 14, 1930.

Bb–19495–2	Sunshine	HMV FJ–133
Bb–19552–2	Banditlied (The Prisoner's Song)	–
Bb–19553–1	The Lonesome Road	HMV FJ–97
Bb–19554–1	Kleine Maat (Little Pal)	–
Bb–19555–2	Ou Kaapstad is mij Hemel-Land	HMV FJ–100

NOTE: All but the first title of this session are sung in Afrikaans.

With THE ALDWYCH PLAYERS, directed by Jay Wilbur.

London, August 2, 1930.

945–1	On The Sunny Side Of The Street	Victory 253 (7″)
946–1	Sweepin' The Clouds Away	Victory 254 (7″)
948–2	Song Of The Dawn (with Hubert Wallace)	Victory 252 (7″)
949–1	Dancing With Tears In My Eyes	Victory 255 (7″)

NOTE: Matrix 947 has a vocal refrain by Hubert Wallace only.

With AL VOCALE AND HIS CROONERS. (NOTE: This, according to Edgar Jackson, in *The Gramophone* for November 1930, is a pseudonym for Len Fillis. Mr Jackson quotes the full personnel of the group, including Al Bowlly and Les Allen as the vocalists, but on none of the four titles listed is this discography is there any singing readily identifiable as that of Al Bowlly).

London, early September 1930.

89867–2	Falling In Love Again (with Les Allen)	EBR 1389 (8″)
89868–2	Say A Little Prayer For Me (w. L.A.)	EBR 1416 (8″)
89869–2	One Night Alone With You (w. Les Allen)	EBR 1389 (8″)

With HAWAIIAN QUARTET (a LEN FILLIS group).

London, September 9, 1930.

| MB–1798–1, –2 | Aloha Oe | Dec rejected |
| MB–1799–1, –2 | Goodbye To All That (with Les Allen) | – |

With LINN MILFORD AND HIS HAWAIIAN PLAYERS.

London, September 19, 1930.

WAR–325–2	Rose Dreams	Re MR–216, G–20931
WAR–326–2	Blue Pacific Moonlight	Re MR–187
WAR–327–2	Here In My Heart	–
WAR–328–2	That Little Lock of Hair	Re MR–216, G–20931

With HAWAIIAN QUARTET.   London, September 24, 1930.

GB–1916–2	There's A Stranger In Heaven Tonight	Dec F–1991
GB–1918–2	Aloha Oe	Dec F–2066
GB–1919–1	Goodbye To All That (w. Les Allen)	Dec F–1958
GB–1921–2	The Golden Gates Of Paradise	Dec F–1991

NOTE: Matrices GB–1917 and GB–1920 are not Al Bowlly items. Decca F–1958 as HONOLULU QUARTET.

Acc. by own gtr., unknown harmonica, concertina and violin, all in Afrikaans.
Hayes, Middlesex, October 10, 1930
Bb-20441-2 Voetslaan op oom Jacob se Leer   HMV FJ-103
Bb-20442-2 Sal die Engele hul Harpe speel vir mij?   –
Bb-20443-2 Daar is geen ron in die Hemel   HMV FJ-120
Bb-20444-2 Die ou lelie Vallei   –

The next session was made under the name of JANNIE VILJOEN, acc. by own gtr. and probably Claude Ivy (pno.). All titles are sung in Taal dialect.
London, October 13, 1930.
GB-2049-1, -2, -3 Minnaarslaan (Sweetheart Lane)   Dec rejected
GB-2050-1, -2 In die Droomvallei (In The Valley Of Dreams)   –
GB-2051-1, -2 Hoe gaan dit (How Do You Do?)   –
GB-2052-1, -2 By die Vaal Rivier (By The Vaal River)   –

With AL VOCALE AND HIS CROONERS.   London, mid-October 1930.
89919-1 Waiting For That Thing Called Happiness (with Les Allen)   EB R 1416 (8")
NOTE: Nothing else was made at this session.

With ALFREDO AND HIS BAND.   London, c October 17, 1930.
13073-2 Great Day (with Les Allen)   EBW 5187
13074-2 Without A Song (with Les Allen)   –
13075-2 Living In The Sunlight, Loving In The Moonlight (with Les Allen)   EBW 5188
13076-2 You Brought A New Kind Of Love To Me (with Les Allen)   –

With JAY WILBUR AND HIS BAND.   London, late October, 1930.
5516 Adeline (with chorus)   Imp 2355

The next session was also made under the name of JANNIE VILJOEN, acc. by own gtr., probably Claude Ivy (pno.) and unknown concertina and harmonica. All titles are sung in Afrikaans.   London, October 30, 1930.
FGB-2156-1, -2, -3 Sy was arm maar sy was eirlik (She Was Poor But She Was Honest)   Dec rejected
FGB-2157-1, -2 Awend (Evening)   –
FGB-2158-1, -2 Woorhuis (Homestead)   –
FGB-2159-1, -2 Ek dink altyd aan jou (I'm Forever Thinking Of You)   –

With THE PHANTOM PLAYERS (Len Fillis and his Band, according to the original recording sheet).   London, November 3, 1930.
GB-2177-2 Lonely Little Vagabond   Dec F-2144
GB-2178-1 She's My Secret Passion   –
NOTE: Two other titles from this session were issued (Decca F-2078), with vocal refrain by Ella Logan on one and no vocal at all on the other.

With EARL MELVILLE AND HIS HAWAIIANS (a LEN FILLIS group).
London, early November, 1930.
3961-2 That's My Song Of Love (w. unknown) Pic 673
3962   That Little Lock Of Hair (My Mother
        Gave To Me) (with unknown)   –
3963   She's My Secret Passion   Pic 649
3964-2 Lonely Little Vagabond   –
3965   There's A Stranger In Heaven Tonight Pic 685

With the HAWAIIAN SERENADERS (probably identifiable with the last group).
London, November 13, 1930.
1040-1 Old Spanish Moon   Victory 302 (7")
1041-2 Love Never Dies   Victory 297 (7")
1042-1 Why Did You Turn Me Down?   Victory 300 (7")
1043-1 Lullaby Land   Victory 301 (?) (7")
1044-1 Love Birds Are Better Than Bluebirds Victory 298 (7")
1054-1 Headin' For Hollywood   Victory 303 (7")
NOTE: We are assuming that 1043-1 was issued on Victory 301, as this is the only Victory record of the period which we have never seen. Should it prove to be some other title, it is reasonable to assume that 1043-1 was rejected.

With EDGAR ADELER'S HAWAIIAN PLAYERS. London, November 1930.
S-1154-1 Sleepy Head   Sterno 594
S-1156-1 With My Guitar And You (w. Les Allen) Sterno 604
S-1157-1 Go Home And Tell Your Mother (w. Les Allen) –
NOTE: Matrix S-1155 has not been traced.

With FERRACHINI'S HAWAIIAN BAND (probably a LEN FILLIS group).
London, November, 1930.
LO-797 Moonlight On The Colorado (with Les Bcst 2605, 3018
        Allen)
LO-798 Cuban Love Song (with Les Allen)   –
Z-1748 The Kiss Waltz (with Les Allen)   Bcst 643 (8")
Z-1749 With My Guitar And You (with Les Allen) –
Z-1750 Bye Bye Blues (with Les Allen)   Bcst 644 (8")
Z-1751 Old New England Moon (with Les Allen) –
NOTE: Broadcasts 643 and 644 are labelled THE WAIKIKI SERENADERS, and were part of a special issue released on December 12, 1930.

With MARIUS B. WINTER AND HIS DANCE ORCHESTRA.
London, November 1930.
LO-801 What A Perfect Night For Love   Bcst 2599
LO-802 Beware Of Love   Bcst 2600

With THE NEW MAYFAIR DANCE ORCHESTRA, directed by Ray Noble.
London, November 20, 1930
Bb-21005-2 I'm Telling The World She's Mine   HMV B-5940, Vic 24752
Bb-21006-1 How Could I Be Lonely?   –   –
NOTE: Victor as RAY NOBLE AND HIS ORCHESTRA.

Acc. by own gtr.-1, Claude Ivy (pno.)-5. London, November 24, 1930.
GB-2322-2 Nigger Blues-1   Dec F-2560
GB-2323-1 Frankie And Johhny-1 (with Ella   Dec F-2206
           Logan)
GB-2324-2 By The Old Oak Tree-1, 5 (with E. Logan) –

With THE BLUE JAYS (EBW 5202) or THE RADIO MELODY BOYS (EBW) 5203, directed by Harry Hudson.   London, c December 1, 1930.
13163-1 What A Perfect Night For Love (with   EBW 5202
         Les Allen)
13164-2 The 'Free And Easy' (with Les Allen) –
13165-1 My Cradle Is The Desert (w. Les Allen) EBW 5203
13166-1 A Japanese Dream (with Les Allen)   –

With MARIUS B. WINTER AND HIS DANCE ORCHESTRA.
                                       London, December 1930.
LO-820   Never Swat A Fly   Bcst 2606
LO-821   Sunny Days (with unknown)   Bcst 2607
LO-822   Roamin' Thru' The Roses   –

With LINN MILFORD AND HIS HAWAIIAN PLAYERS.
                                       London, December 17, 1930.
WAR-450-1 There's A Stranger In Heaven   Re MR-267, G-20989
           Tonight
WAR-451-2 Sleepy Head   Re MR-337
WAR-452-2 In An Old Churchyard   –
WAR-453-2 The Silver-Toned Chimes Of The Re MR-267, G-20989
           Angelus

With THE PALM BEACH HAWAIIANS (probably a LEN FILLIS group).
                                       London, December 18, 1930.
GB-2415-2 That's What Loneliness Means To Me Dec F-2246

With BILLY HILL AND HIS BOYS.   London, December 18, 1930.
GB-2416-2 The Farmyard Symphony   Dec F-2172
GB-2417-1, -2 When Bill Malone Plays The   Rejected
           Xylophone
GB-2418-2 The Village Jazz Band   Dec F-2172

With THE RADIO MELODY BOYS (EBR 1447) or THE BLUE JAYS (EBR 1448), directed by Harry Hudson.   London, December 30, 1930.
89986-1 My Sunshine Came On A Rainy Day   EBR 1447
         (with Les Allen)
89987-1 Underneath The Spanish Stars (with L. Allen) –
89988-2 A Little Love Song (with Les Allen)   EBR 1448
89989-2 Okay, Baby (with Les Allen)   –

With THE NEW MAYFAIR DANCE ORCHESTRA, directed by Ray Noble.
                                       London, December 31, 1930.
Bb-21107-1 Underneath The Spanish Stars   HMV B-5955

Bb-21108-2	Sunny Days	HMV B-5956
Bb-21109-2	Make Yourself A Happiness Pie	HMV B-5957

With ROY FOX AND HIS BAND. (NOTE: All Roy Fox's records mentioned in this book bear on the labels the legend 'At The Monseigneur Restaurant, London'.) London, January 5, 1931.

GB-2498-2	Memories Of You	Dec F-2194
GB-2499-1	You're Lucky To Me	–
GB-2500-2	Thank Your Father	Dec F-2312

With THE BLUE JAYS (EBR 1456) or HARRY HUDSON'S MELODY MEN (EBR 1458), directed by Harry Hudson. London, *c* January 9, 1931.

90012-2	Old-Fashioned Girl (with Les Allen)	EBR 1456
90013-2	Never Swat A Fly (with Les Allen)	–
90014-2	Sweet Jennie Lee (with Les Allen)	EBR 1458
90015-2	You're Driving Me Crazy (with Les Allen)	–

With ROY FOX AND HIS BAND. London, January 16, 1931.

GB-2519-3	Can't We Be Friends?	Dec F-2220

With FERROCHINI'S HAWAIIAN BAND. London, January, 1931.

LO-845	My Bluebird Was Caught In The Rain	Bcst 3008
LO-846	Somewhere In Old Wyoming (with Les Allen)	–
Z-1831	Oh Donna Clara! (with Les Allen)	Bcst 673 (8")
Z-1832	Nobody Cares If I'm Blue (with Les Allen)	–

With MARIUS B. WINTER AND HIS DANCE ORCHESTRA.
London, January 1931.

LO-848	There's Something About An Old-Fashioned Girl	Bcst 3003
LO-850	A Little Love Song	Bcst 3004

NOTE: The vocalist on matrices LO-847 and LO-849 is not Al Bowlly.

With THE PALM BEACH HAWAIIANS. London, January 23, 1931.

GB-2545-1	Somewhere In Old Wyoming (with Allen)	Dec F-2213
GB-2546-2	Oh! Donna Clara (with Les Allen)	–
GB-2548-1	Hurt	Dec F-2317

NOTE: Matric GB-2547 has a vocal refrain by Les Allen only.

With ROY FOX AND HIS BAND. London, January 24, 1931.

GB-2549-3	Wedding Bells Are Ringing For Sally	Dec F-2219
GB-2550-2	Missouri Waltz	Dec F-2233
GB-2551-3	Lady, Play Your Mandoline	Dec F-2220

London, January 28, 1931.

GB-2579-3	Hurt	Dec F-2239
GB-2580-3	Writing A Letter To You	Dec F-2249
GB-2581-4	A Peach Of A Pair	Dec F-2233

London, February 9, 1931.

GB-2684-1	Between The Devil And The Deep Blue Sea (with chorus)	Dec F-2240
GB-2685-2	The Peanut Vendor (with chorus)	Dec F-2239
GB-2686-1	Maybe It's Love (with chorus)	Dec F-2240

With THE PALM BEACH HAWAIIANS.   London, February 9, 1931.

GB-2690-1	'Neath Hawaiian Skies	Dec F-2255
GB-2691-	Really Mine	Dec F-2246

The following record has been mentioned as being an Al Bowlly item. We have not yet been able to hear it.

With THE RADIO RHYTHM BOYS, directed by Harry Hudson.

London, February 1931.

90060-1	Tap Your Feet	EBR 1489 (8″)
90061-2	Makin' Wicki-Wacki Down In Waikiki	–

With THE NEW MAYFAIR DANCE ORCHESTRA, directed by Ray Noble.

London, February 19, 1931.

OB-368-1	Time On My Hands	HMV B-5983, Vic 25016
OB-369-3	Makin' Wickey-Wackey Down In Waikiki	HMV B-4989, EA-902
OB-370-3	Shout For Happiness	HMV B-5984
OB-371-2	Goodnight, Sweetheart	– EA-908, Vic 25016, 20-2950
OB-372-1	I'm Glad I Waited	HMV B-5983
OB-373-2	Really Mine	HMV B-5989, EA-902
OB-374-4	Puzzle Record No. 1—Part 2 (Al Bowlly sings a chorus of 'You're Driving Me Crazy')	HMV B-3775, Vic 22745

NOTE: HMV B-3775 and Victor 22745 as NOVELTY ORCHESTRA.

With ROY FOX AND HIS BAND.   London, February 26, 1931.

GB-2700-1	You're The One I Care For	Dec F-2256
GB-2701-2	Overnight	–
GB-2702-2	Shout! For Happiness	Dec F-2263

With THE BLUE JAYS, directed by Harry Hudson.

London, c March 3, 1931.

13339-2	Sweet Jennie Lee (with Les Allen)	EBW 5242
13340-2	Ti-dle-id-dle-um-pum (with Les Allen)	–

With ROY FOX AND HIS BAND.   London, March 5, 1931.

GB-2715-3	When Your Hair Has Turned To Silver	Dec F-2263
GB-2716-2	Bathing In The Sunshine	Dec F-2250
GB-2717-3	Reaching For The Moon	Dec F-2279
GB-2718-1	All Through The Night	Dec F-2249

With NOVELTY ORCHESTRA, directed by Ray Noble.

London, March 9, 1931.

OB–145–1 Puzzle Record No. 2—Part 1   HMV B–3825
    (Al Bowlly sings a chorus of 'I'll be Good Because Of You')
OB–146–4 Puzzle Record No. 2—Part 2   HMV B–3825
    (Al Bowlly sings a chorus of 'Goodnight, Sweetheart')

With ROY FOX AND HIS BAND.   London, March 10, 1931.

GB–2725–2 Them There Eyes (with two others)   Dec F–2252
GB–2726–2 That Lindy Hop   Dec F–2250
GB–2727–3 Truly (with chorus)   Dec F–2292

London, March 13, 1931.

GB–2731–1 I'm Glad I Waited   Dec F–2291
    NOTE: Matrix GB–2730 has no vocal refrain by Al Bowlly.

With THE NEW MAYFAIR DANCE ORCHESTRA (HMV B–5999) or NEW MAYFAIR ORCHESTRA (HMV B–3836), directed by Ray Noble

London, March 24, 1931.

OB–680–3 Pages Of Radioland—Part 1   HMV B–3836
    (Al Bowlly sings a chorus of 'Without A Song')
OB–681–2 Pages Of Radioland—Part 2   HMV B–3836
    (Al Bowlly sings a chorus of 'Falling In Love Again')
OB–682–1 We Two   HMV B–5999, EA–908
OB–683–3 Lady Of Spain   – EA–978, Vic 22774, 24499

    NOTE: Victors as LONDON MAYFAIR ORCHESTRA.

With ROY FOX AND HIS BAND.   London, March 25, 1931.

GB–2751–3 One More Time   Dec F–2294
GB–2752–2 Lady Of Spain   Dec F–2279
GB–2753–1 Time On My Hands   Dec F–2291

With THE NEW MAYFAIR DANCE ORCHESTRA, directed by Ray Noble.

London, March 26, 1931.

OB–694–1 Sunshine And Shadows   HMV B–6010

With MARIUS B. WINTER AND HIS DANCE ORCHESTRA.

London, late March 1931.

LO–880   All Through The Night   Bcst 3034
    NOTE: The vocalist on matrix LO–879, the reverse of the above, is not Al Bowlly.

With THE RADIO MELODY BOYS, directed by Harry Hudson.

London, late March 1931.

90079–2 Maybe It's Love (with Les Allen)   EBR 1478 (8")
90080–2 Beyond The Blue Horizon   –

With ROY FOX AND HIS BAND.   London, April 1, 1931.

GB–2760–2 Alma Mia (with trio)   Dec F–2292
GB–2761–2 Koppa-Ka-Banna (with trio)   Dec F–2315

                            London, April 15, 1931.
GB-2773-2 Betty Co-Ed   Dec F-2312
GB-2774-3 You Didn't Have To Tell Me Dec F-2318
GB-2775-3 When It's Sunset On The Nile Dec F-2315
                            London, April 21, 1931.
GB-2784-2 Would You Like To Take A Walk? Dec F-2318
GB-2785-2 Laughing At The Rain   Dec F-2328
GB-2786-3 Ya Got Love   Dec F-2329
GB-2787-2 Bubbling Over With Love   Dec F-2328

With PERCY CHANDLER AND HIS BAND. London, late April, 1931.
  4309   Why Couldn't You?   Pic 789
  4310, -2 Tango Lady   Pic 764, Empire E-7,
                                     May G-2031, Oct 608
  4311   Really Mine   Pic 764
  NOTE: Empire as ALBERTA DANCE BAND; Mayfair as ARGENTINE TANGO ORCHESTRA.

With THE NEW MAYFAIR DANCE ORCHESTRA, directed by Ray Noble.
                            London, April 28, 1931.
OB-799-3   That's Somerset   HMV B-6011
OB-800-2   Fiesta   HMV B-6010
OB-801-2   You're Twice As Nice As The Girl In HMV B-6011, EA-923
           My Dreams

With ROY FOX AND HIS BAND.   London, May 5, 1931.
GB-2805-1 Fiesta   Dec F-2341
GB-2806-3 By My Side   —
GB-2807-1 My Temptation   Dec F-2329

With LEN FILLIS AND HIS NOVELTY ORCHESTRA.
                            London, May 6, 1931.
A-11565-1 Song Hits—Part 1 (with Les Allen)   Col DB-516
           (Bowlly and Allen sing a duet chorus of 'Reaching For The Moon')
A-11566-1 Song Hits—Part 4   Col DB-549
           (Al Bowlly sings a chrous of 'Bubbling Over With Love')
A-11567-1 Song Hits—Part 3 (with Les Allen)   Col DB-549
           (Bowlly and Allen sing a chorus of 'Lady Of Spain')
A-11568-1 Song Hits—Part 2 (with Les Allen)   Col DB-516
           (Bowlly and Allen singing a chorus of 'Hawaiian Stars Are Gleaming')

With THE NEW MAYFAIR DANCE ORCHESTRA (HMV B-6023, Victor 24004), or NEW MAYFAIR ORCHESTRA (HMV B-3881) directed by Ray Noble.
                            London, May 29, 1931.
OB-949-2   On With The Show—Part 1   HMV B-3881
           (Al Bowlly sings a chorus of 'On A Little Balcony in Spain')

OB–950–2	Lights Of Paris	HMV B–6023, Vic 24004
OB–951–3	June-Time Is Love Time	–
OB–952–1	On With The Show—Part 2	HMV B–3881

(Al Bowlly sings a chorus of 'Pretty Kitty Kelly')

With ROY FOX AND HIS BAND.   London, June 1, 1931.

GB–2852–3	I'm So Used To You Now	Dec F–2352★
GB–2853–3	I'm Gonna Get You	Dec F–2351★
GB–2854–1	It Must Be True	– ★
GB–2855–2	Leave The Rest To Nature	Dec F–2352★

NOTE: Memo from the Chenil Galleries studios: 'Vocal Refrain by A Bowlly—type to be as large as possible.'

With THE WALDORFIANS, directed by Howard Godfrey.

London, early June, 1931.

| 4360–2 | My Canary Has Circles Under His Eyes | Pic 780, May M1–2019, Simcha 10002 |
| 4361–2 | Miss Elizabeth Brown | – Empire E–12 – |

NOTE: Empire as BASIL WINSTON AND HIS BAND; Mayfair as FIFTH AVENUE DANCE BAND; Simcha as COSMOPOLITAN SYNCOPATORS.

With JACK LEON AND HIS BAND.   London, early June, 1931.

4362	Lights Of Paris	Pic 782, Oct 614
4363–2	Bell-Bottom Trousers	– –
		Simcha 10001
4364, –2	Ya Got Love	Pic 783
4365	Walking My Baby Back Home	– Empire E–12, Simcha 10001

NOTE: Empire as ALBERTA DANCE BAND; Simcha as JEROME JOY AND HIS BAND.

With THE WALDORFIANS, directed by Howard Godfrey.

London, early June, 1931.

4366–2	Thank You Most Sincerely	Pic 781, Oct 613
		Simcha 10002
4367–2	Life Is Meant For Love	– –
4368–2	Time On My Hands	Pic 787, Oct 617, Empire E–9

NOTE: Empire as BASIL WINSTON AND HIS ORCHESTRA; Simcha as THE COSMOPOLITAN SYNCOPATORS.

With THE BLUE JAYS (EBR 1507) or RADIO RHYTHM BOYS (EBR 1508), directed by Harry Hudson.   London, early June, 1931.

| 90158–1 | Walkin' My Baby Back Home | EBR 1507 (8″) |
| 90160–1 | Let's Get Friendly | EBR 1508 (8″) |

NOTE: Matrices 90159 and 90161, which are on the reverse of EBR 1507 and 1508 respectively, do not have vocal refrains by Al Bowlly.

With THE DEAUVILLE DANCE BAND, directed by Harry Hudson.
          London, early June, 1931.
 13553-2 Time On My Hands   EBW 5315
 13554-2 I'm Glad I Waited   –
Acc. by Claude Ivy (pno.)   London, June 10, 1931.
GB-2875-2 I'm So Used To You Now Dec F-2366
GB-2876-1 Leave The Rest To Nature –
With THE NEW MAYFAIR DANCE ORCHESTRA, directed by Ray Noble.
          London, June 11, 1931.
OB-976-3 Roll On, Mississippi, Roll On (with HMV B-6040
    The Three Ginx)
OB-977-2 Lazy Day   HMV B-6031
OB-978-4 I'd Rather Be A Beggar With You HMV B-6040, EA-956
 NOTE: The vocalist on OB-975-2 is not Al Bowlly.
With ROY FOX AND HIS BAND. London, June 16, 1931.
GB-2906-1 Lazy Day   Dec F-2396★
GB-2907-2 Poor Kid   – ★
GB-2908-1, -2, -3 By The River Sainte Marie Rejected
With JACK LEON AND HIS BAND. London, mid-June, 1931.
 4372-2 Leave The Rest To Nature Pic 796
 4373 I'm So Used To You Now –
 4374-2 Goodnight, Sweetheart   Pic 787, Oct 617
          London, late June, 1931.
 4383-2 Shake And Let Us Be Friends Pic 802
 4384-2 I'll Keep You In My Heart Always Pic 788
 4385-2 Oh! Rosalita   –
 4386-2 Bubbling Over With Love Pic 802
 4387 I Offer You These Roses   Pic 799
With THE NEW MAYFAIR ORCHESTRA, directed by Ray Noble.
          London, June 26, 1931.
OB-1243-3 Miracle Melodies—Part 1 HMV B-3907
   (Al Bowlly sings a chorus of 'Goodnight, Sweetheart')
OB-1245-1 Holiday Hits—Part 1   HMV B-3910
   (Al Bowlly sings a chorus of 'Reaching For The Moon')
OB-1246-1 Holiday Hits—Part 2   HMV B-3910
   (Al Bowlly sings a chorus of 'River, Stay 'Way From My
   Door')
With MAURICE WINNICK AND HIS ORCHESTRA.
          London, July 10, 1931.
CAR-740-1 Topical Tunes Medley—Part 1 Re MR-374
   (Al Bowlly sings a chorus of 'What A Fool I've Been')
CAR-741-1 Springtime Reminds Me Of You Re MR-375
CAR-742-1 The Waltz You Saved For Me –

CAR-743-1   Topical Tunes Medley—Part 2   Re MR-374
            (Al Bowlly sings a chorus of 'Pardon Me, Pretty Baby')
With THE NEW MAYFAIR ORCHESTRA, directed by Ray Noble.
                                     London, July 14, 1931.
OB-1284-2   Tunes Of Not-So-Long-Ago—1921   HMV B-3944
            (Al Bowlly sings a chorus of 'Coal Black Mammy and 'Swanee')
OB-1285-2   Tunes Of Not-So-Long-Ago—1923   HMV B-4012
            (Al Bowlly sings a chorus of 'My Sweetie Went Away' and
            'Yes! We Have No Bananas')
With ROY FOX AND HIS BAND.   London, July 21, 1931.
GB-3026-2   When You Were The Blossom Of   Dec F-2403★ +
            Buttercup Lane
GB-3027-1, -3   Tie A Little String Around Your Finger -   ★
GB-3028-2   I Found You   Dec F-2404★
GB-3029-1   Love For Sale   –
  NOTE: Although there is no vocal refrain as such on 'Love For Sale', due to
  the ban on the lyrics, Al Bowlly can be heard humming on this side.
With ROLANDO'S SALON ORCHESTRA.   London, c late July, 1931.
13708-2   Goodnight   EBW 5361
  NOTE: Matrix 13709, which is on the reverse of the above, has a vocal
  refrain by Sam Browne.
With ROY FOX AND HIS BAND.   London, July 31, 1931.
GB-3090-3   Roll On, Mississippi, Roll On   Dec F-2438★
GB-3091-1   Out Of Nowhere   Dec F-2439★
GB-3092-1   While Hearts Are Singing   –   ★
GB-3093-1   I'd Rather Be A Beggar With You Dec F-2438★, F-2609★
With THE RADIO MELODY BOYS (EBR 1535) or THE BLUE JAYS (EBR 1541),
  directed by Harry Hudson.   London, early August, 1931.
90207-2   Belle Of Barcelona   EBR 1535 (8")
90208-1   I'm A Hundred Per Cent. In Love With You –
90209-1   Poor Kid   EBR 1541 (8")
90210-2   Mama Inez   –
With THE NEW MAYFAIR DANCE ORCHESTRA, directed by Ray Noble.
                                     London, August 14, 1931.
OB-1314-1   Pagan Serenade   HMV B-6055
OB-1315-2   Belle Of Barcelona   –   EA-958
OB-1316-2   There's Something In Your Eyes   HMV B-6056   –
OB-1317-2   Just A Dancing Sweetheart   –
  NOTE: Some copies of the fourth title above are labelled 'Only A Dancing
  Sweetheart'.
With ROY FOX AND HIS BAND.   London, August 18, 1931.
GB-3134-1   Tell Me, Are You From Georgia?   Dec F-2451★
            (with Nat Gonella)

128

GB-3135-1   You Are My Heart's Delight   Dec F-2469★
GB-3137-1   Cherie, c'est vous   Dec F-2451★
   NOTE: Matrix GB-3136 is 'Whispering', Roy Fox's famous signature tune, and the only voice heard on it is his, introducing the title.

With THE NEW MAYFAIR DANCE ORCHESTRA, directed by Ray Noble.
                                      London, August 25, 1931.
OB-1330-2   When It's Sunset On The Nile   HMV B-6057, EA-972
OB-1331-2   Honeymoon Lane   HMV B-6058   –
OB-1333-2   Hang Out The Stars In Indiana   –   Vic 24357
   NOTE: The vocalist on OB-1332, the reverse of HMV B-6057, is not Al Bowlly.

With SID PHILLIPS AND HIS MELODIANS.   London, late August, 1931.
   13772-1, -2   Roll On, Mississippi, Roll On   EBW 5358
   13773-1   Heartaches   –
   13774-1   Time Alone Will Tell   EBW 5356
   13775-2   Tell Me You Love Me   –

Acc. by orchestra.   London, September 2, 1931.
GB-3168-1   Were You Sincere?   Dec F-2485
GB-2169-2   I'd Rather Be A Beggar With You   –

With ROY FOX AND HIS BAND.   London, September 3, 1931.
GB-3170-2   You Can't Stop Me From Loving   Dec F-2487
            You
GB-3172-1, -2   Dance Hall Doll   Dec F-2486
GB-3173-2   What Are You Thinking About, Baby?   –
   NOTE: Neither of the voices on matrix GB-3171 is Al Bowlly's.

With THE DEAUVILLE DANCE BAND (EBR 1550) or THE RADIO RHYTHM BOYS (EBR 1551), directed by Harry Hudson. London, September, 1931.
   90225-1   Roll On, Mississippi, Roll On   EBR 1550 (8″)
   90226-1   Wrap Your Troubles In Dreams   –
   90227-2   Honeymoon Lane   EBR 1551 (8″)
   90228-2   I Can't Do Without You (with chorus)   –

With ROY FOX AND HIS BAND.   London, September 18, 1931.
GB-3277-1   Time Alone Will Tell   Dec F-2513
GB-3278-2   When The Waltz Was Through   –
GB-3279-1   Sing Another Chorus, Please   Dec F-2514
GB-3280-1   Sweet And Lovely   –

With THE BLUE JAYS (EBR 1556) or THE DEAUVILLE DANCE BAND (EBR 1558), directed by Harry Hudson.   London, c late September, 1931.
   90237-1   By The River Sainte Marie   EBR 1558 (8″)
   90238-1   I'm Thru' With Love   –
   90239-2   Hang Out The Stars In Indiana   EBR 1556 (8″)
   90240-3   Just One More Chance   –

129

With ROY FOX AND HIS BAND.　　　London, October 2, 1931.
GB–3349–2　Looking For You　　　Dec F–2574
GB–3350–1　Kiss Me Goodnight　　　Dec F–2581
GB–3351–3　Song Of Happiness　　　Dec F–2574

　　　　　　　　　　　　London, October 7, 1931.
GB–3387–2　Just One More Chance　　　Dec F–2580
GB–3388–2　Smile, Darn Ya, Smile　　　–
GB–3389–2　That's What I Like About You　　　Dec F–2581
GB–3390–2　You Forgot Your Gloves　　　Dec F–2582
GB–3391–2　Take It From Me (I'm Taking To You)　　　–

　　　　　　　　　　　　London, October 16, 1931.
GB–3456–2　Yes, Yes (My Baby Said Yes)　　　Dec F–2609
GB–3457–1, –2, –3　You Call It Madness　　　Rejected
GB–3458–1　I Found A Million-Dollar Baby (In　　　Dec F–2610
　　　　　　A Five-And-Ten-Cent Store)
GB–2459–1　Look In The Looking-Glass　　　–

With the SAVOY HOTEL ORPHEANS.　　　London, October 19, 1931.
CA–12092　There's A Time And Place For　　　Col CB–376, DO–618
　　　　　　Everything
CA–12093　Sweet And Lovely　　　–

　　　　　　　　　　　　London, October 31, 1931.
CA–12139　Who Am I?　　　Col CB–377
CA–12140　Linda　　　–

With THE NEW MAYFAIR DANCE ORCHESTRA, directed by Ray Noble.
　　　　　　　　　　　　London, October 31, 1931.
OB–1777–2　Down Sunnyside Lane　　　HMV B–6091
OB–1778–1　This Is The Day Of Days　　　–

With ROY FOX AND HIS BAND.　　　London, November 5, 1931.
GB–3538–3　This Is The Missus　　　Dec F–2682
GB–3539–3　Over The Blue　　　Dec F–2683
GB–3540–2　'Neath The Spell Of Monte Carlo　　　–
GB–3541–2　Life Is Just A Bowl Of Cherries　　　Dec F–2682

With THE NEW MAYFAIR DANCE ORCHESTRA, directed by Ray Noble.
　　　　　　　　　　　　London, November 14, 1931.
OB–2228–2　Got A Date With An Angel　　　HMV B–6098, EA–991,
　　　　　　　　　　　　　　　　　　Vic 22953
OB–2229–1, –2　Guilty　　　HMV B–6097
OB–2231–2　Twentieth Century Blues　　　HMV B–4001, K–6979,
　　　　　　　　　　　　　　　　　　El EG–2930, Vic 24090

NOTE: All issues of the last title as NEW MAYFAIR NOVELTY ORCHESTRA, which consists only of trumpet, clarinet, and piano duet by Ray Noble and Harry Jacobson. Matrix OB–2230 has no vocal refrain at all.

With HOWARD GODFREY AND HIS WALDORFIANS.
London, November, 1931.

4509	Looking For You	Pic 849, Oct 133
4510	That's What I Like About You	–
4511–2	Got A Date With An Angel	Pic 855, Oct 133
4512	The Way With Every Sailor	Pic 856, Oct 134
4513	Who Do You Love?	Pic 855 –
4514–2	Over The Blue	Pic 856

With THE DEAUVILLE DANCE BAND (EBR 1584) or THE BLUE JAYS (EBR 1585), directed by Harry Hudson.   London, November, 1931.

90279–1	Lies	EBR 1584 (8")
90280–3	Rio de Janeiro	–
90281–2	Linda	EBR 1585 (8")
90282–2	Dear, When I Met You	–

With BILLY COTTON AND HIS BAND.   London, December 1, 1931.
CAR–896–1   I Can't Get Mississippi Off My Mind Re MR–463

NOTE: None of the other three titles from this session has a vocal refrain by Al Bowlly. A test pressing of CAR–896–2 exists, also featuring him, with an excellent trumpet obbligato. It is not known if this was used for issue.

With RAY NOBLE AND THE NEW MAYFAIR DANCE ORCHESTRA.
London, December 1, 1931.
OB–2031–5   Hold My Hand   HMV B–6112,
                                   El EG–2513, Vic 24034

With ROY FOX AND HIS BAND.   London, December 2, 1931.

GB–3456–4	Yes, Yes (My Baby Said Yes)	Dec F–2720
GB–3457–5	You Call It Madness (But I Call It Love)	–
GB–3664–1	Nobody's Sweetheart	Dec F–2716
GB–3665–1	Guilty	–

With RAY NOBLE AND THE NEW MAYFAIR DANCE ORCHESTRA.
London, December 4, 1931.
OB–2484–4   Pied Piper Of Hamelin   HMV B–6112, Vic 24034

NOTE: None of the other titles from this or its partner-date (December 1, 1931) has a vocal refrain by Al Bowlly.

With THE TUFF GUYS, a vocal and instrumental group directed by Harry Hudson.
London, December 9, 1931.
90297–1   Eleven More Months And Ten More   EBR 1586 (8")
          Days

Acc. by THE RADIO RHYTHM FIVE, probably the same group as the Tuff Guys.
London, December 9, 1931.

| 14044–2 | Eleven More Months And Ten More Days | EBW 5440 |
| 14045–2 | Foolish Facts | – |

With RAY NOBLE AND THE NEW MAYFAIR DANCE ORCHESTRA.
London, December 19, 1931.
OB-2518-3 I Was True (with chorus)   HMV B-6118
OB-2519-2 One Little Quarrel   —

With ROY FOX AND HIS BAND.   London, December 30, 1931.
GB-3761-1 The Longer That You Linger In   Dec F-2760
           Virginia
GB-3762-1, -2 There's Something In Your Eyes Rejected
GB-3768-1 If I Didn't Have You   Dec F-2763, M-1083
  NOTE: Matrices GB-3763/6 inclusive are by other artists; GB-3767 is 'Oh Mo'-Nah!' with vocal refrain by Nat Gonella and chorus (which may include Bowlly but not obviously).

With JOCK MCDERMOTT AND HIS BAND.   London, c January 5, 1932.
14114-1 Mona Lisa   EBW 5458
14115-1 Hold My Hand   —
14116-2 Whispering   EBW 5468
14117-3 Dinah   —

With ROY FOX AND HIS BAND.   London, January 7, 1932
GB-3762-4 There's Something In Your Eyes Dec F-2760
GB-3781-1, -2 Prisoner Of Love   Rejected
GB-3782-1, -2 You Didn't Know The Music
  NOTE: Matrices GB-3779/80 have vocal refrains by others than Al Bowlly.

With the SAVOY HOTEL ORPHEANS.   London, January 7, 1932.
CA-12341-3 You're The Kind Of A Baby For Me Col CB-403
  NOTE: Matrix CA-12342 has a vocal refrain by Jack Plant.

With RAY NOBLE AND THE NEW MAYFAIR DANCE ORCHESTRA.
London, January 8, 1932.
OB-2102-3 Put Your Ltitle Arms Around Me   HMV B-6131, EA-1079
OB-2103-2 Meet Me Tonight In The Cowshed   HMV B-6130
           (dialogue with Leonard Henry)
OB-2104-1 By The Fireside   HMV B-6131, EA-1077,
                                            Vic 25141
OB-2105-2 Must It End Like This?   HMV B-6130

Acc. by pno. (probably Harry Hudson).   London, c January 13, 1932.
14126-1 A Faded Summer Love   EBW 5470
14127-1 You Didn't Know The Music —

With THE MASQUERADERS.   London, January 14, 1932.
CA-12349-1 Actions Speak Louder Than Words Col CB-409
CA-12351-   One Little Quarrel (w. Anona Winn) Col CB-413
  NOTE: Matrix CA-12350 has a vocal refrain by Anona Winn only; it is on the reverse of Columbia CB-413. The reverse of CB-409 has a vocal refrain (by Jack Plant), but it was made at a different session.

With ROY FOX AND HIS BAND. London, January 21, 1932.
GB-3781-4 Prisoner Of Love   Dec F-2775
GB-3782-4 You Didn't Know The Music –
GB-3854-2 To Be Worthy Of You   Dec F-2793, M-1018
GB-3855-1 Jig Time   –

With THE RHYTHM MANIACS (on this occasion, a psuedonym for Roy Fox's Band!). London, January 28, 1932.
GB-3889-2 If Anything Happened To You Dec F-3086
GB-3890-2 In London On A Night Like This –

With THE NEW CUMBERLAND DANCE ORCHESTRA.
                                      London, c January, 1932.
1910 Falling In Love   Film 378
1912 You Call It Madness   Film 379
1915 I Idolize My Baby's Eyes   Film 378
1916 Life Is Just A Bowl Of Cherries Film 379
NOTE: Matrices 1911, 1913 and 1914 are still untraced.

With ROY FOX AND HIS BAND. London, February 4, 1932.
GB-3922-3 Adios   Dec F-2805, M-1017
NOTE: Al Bowlly's vocal contribution to this title consists of singing the word 'Adios' twice near the beginning. He does not appear on the other sides made at this session.

With RAY NOBLE AND THE NEW MAYFAIR DANCE ORCHESTRA.
                                      London, February 12, 1932.
OB-2186-2 Sweetheart In My Dreams Tonight HMV B-6146, Vic 24173
OB-2187-2 It's Great To Be In Love   HMV B-6147, EA-1097,
                                             Vic 25232
OB-2188-1 Blues In My Heart   –   El EG-2684,
                                             Vic 25141

With the SAVOY HOTEL ORPHEANS. London, February 16, 1932.
CA-12424-2 Whistling Waltz   Col CB-425, DO-684
CA-12425-2 Sweetheart In My Dreams Tonight –
CA-12426-2 Save The Last Dance For Me   Col CB-426, DO-684

With THE MASQUERADERS. London, February 18, 1932.
CA-12443-2 Granny's Photo Album   Col CB-434, DO-717
CA-12444-2 Kiss By Kiss (with the Carlyle Col CB-429
              Cousins)
CA-12445-1 The Night You Gave Me Back The Ring –
              (with the Carlyle Cousins)
CA-12446-1 Only Me Knows Why   Col CB-428

With ROY FOX AND HIS BAND. London, February 22, 1932.
GB-4012-2 Concentratin'   Dec F-2839
GB-4013-3 Minnie The Moocher (with Lew   Dec F-2834, M-1085
              Stone and Bill Harty)

133

GB-4014-2 Kicking The Gong Around (Al Bowlly – –
           speaks the part of a Chinese)
With RAY NOBLE AND THE NEW MAYFAIR DANCE ORCHESTRA.
                                    London, March 3, 1932.
OB-3008-2 There's A Ring Around The Moon HMV B-6154, EA-1102,
                                                 El EG-2567, Vic 24149
OB-3009-2 With Love In My Heart   HMV B-6157
   NOTE: Al Bowlly does not sing on matrix OB-3010.
With THE MASQUERADERS.   London, March 5, 1932.
CA-12505-1 With Love In My Heart   Col CB-442, DO-718
CA-12506-2 Take Away The Moon   Col CB-435
CA-12507-1 We'll Be Together Again   Col CB-434, DO-717
CA-12508-2 Tell Tales   Col CB-435
With JOHN WATT's 'SONGS FROM THE SHOWS', acc. by orchestra and compered
by John Watt, with Elsie Carlisle.* London, March 7, 1932.
GA-4069-2 Songs From The Shows—Part 1   Dec K-645
           (Al Bowlly sings a chorus of 'It Happened In Monterey')
GA-4070-2 *Songs From The Shows—Part 2   Dec K-645
           (Al Bowlly sings a chorus of 'My Baby Just Cares for Me')
With ROY FOX AND HIS BAND.   London, March 7, 1932.
GB-4071-2 My Sweet Virginia   Dec F-2866, M-1107
GB-4072-1, -2 If I Have To Go On Without You   –   M-1108
GB-4073-3 Kiss By Kiss   Dec F-2867, M-1107
GB-4074-2 Goodnight, Moon   –   M-1108
With THE MASQUERADERS.   London, March 11, 1932.
CA-12527-1 The Cat And The Fiddle—Selection Part 1 (Al Bowlly sings a
           chorus of 'Try To Forget')   Col DB-782, DO-1107
CA-12528-1 The Cat And The Fiddle—Selection Part 2 (Al Bowlly sings a
           chorus of 'She Didn't Say Yes)   Col DB-782, DO-1107
With THE DURIUM DANCE BAND (apparently Roy Fox's Band).
                                    London, mid-March 1932.
E-1003-B All Of Me/Save The Last Dance For Me Durium EN-8
E-1004-B, -C One More Kiss/By The Fireside   Durium EN-9
With ROY FOX AND HIS BAND.   London, March 22, 1932.
GB-4114-1 She Didn't Say Yes (as one of trio) Dec F-2888
GB-4115-2 Goodnight, Vienna   Dec F-2889, Br 6375
GB-4116-2 Living In Clover   –   –
   NOTE: The vocalist on matrix GB-4113 is Eve Becke.
With THE MASQUERADERS.   London, March 24, 1932.
CA-12544-1 The King Was In The Counting-   Col CB-443, DO-719
           House
CA-12545-2 Goopy Gear   Col CB-442, DO-718
CA-12546-1 Sailing On the Robert E. Lee   Col CB-443, DO-719

With RAY NOBLE AND THE NEW MAYFAIR DANCE ORCHESTRA.
                                    London, April 7, 1932.
OB-3063-1   Goodnight, Vienna   HMV B-6172,
                                    El EG-2567, Vic 24064
OB-3064-2   Give Me A Tune   HMV B-6182
OB-3065-2   Living In Clover   HMV B-6172, Vic 24064
With ROY FOX AND HIS BAND.   London, April 13, 1932.
GB-4255-2   Somebody Loves You   Dec F-2922
GB-4256-2   I'm For You A Hundred Per Cent.   Dec F-2923
GB-4257-1, -3   Can't We Talk It Over?   Dec F-2923
GB-4258-2   When We're Alone   Dec F-2922
With THE DURIUM DANCE BAND (apparently Roy Fox's Band).
                                    London, mid-April, 1932.
E-1023-B   Was That The Human Thing To Do?/   Durium EN-11
            Now That You're Gone
E-1024-B, -C   Goodnight, Vienna/My Sweet   Durium EN-9
            Virginia
With RAY NOBLE AND THE NEW MAYFAIR ORCHESTRA (HMV B-6176, B-6203) or the NEW MAYFAIR ORCHESTRA (HMV B-4188), directed by Ray Noble.
                                    London, April 21, 1932.
OB-2860-2   With All My Love And Kisses   HMV B-6176, EA-1123,
                                    Vic 24128
OB-2861-2   We've Got The Moon And Sixpence   HMV B-6203,
                                    El EG-2684, Vic 24212
    NOTE: Matrices 2B-2858/9 have vocal refrains by George Baker.
                                    London, May 3, 1932.
OB-2870-2   One Hour With You—Selection Part 2 (Al Bowlly sings a chorus
            of 'What Would You Do?')   HMV B-4188
OB-2871-1   One Hour With You—Selection Part 1 (Al Bowlly sings a chorus
            of 'One Hour With You')   HMV B-4188
OB-2874-2   Sailing On The Robert E. Lee   HMV B-6176,
                                    El EG-2581, Vic 24128
    NOTE: Cavan O'Connor sings on OB-2872/3.
With ROY FOX AND HIS BAND.   London, May 4, 1932.
GB-4409-2   Lovable   Dec F-2963
GB-4411-2   Love, You Funny Thing   Dec F-2964
GB-4412-2   Getting Sentimental   Dec F-2963
    NOTE: The vocalist on matrix GB-4410 is not Al Bowlly.
With THE DURIUM DANCE BAND (apparently Roy Fox's Band).
                                    London, early May, 1932.
E-1029-A, -C   Can't We Talk It Over?/Just   Durium EN-13
            Humming Along
E-1030-B   Auf Wiedersehen, My Dear/Rain On   Durium EN-12
            The Roof

With the SAVOY HOTEL ORPHEANS.　　London, May 11, 1932.
CA-12691-3　Snuggled On Your Shoulder　　Col CB-458, DO-756
CA-12693-2　When We're Alone　　Col CB-459
CA-12694-1　What Makes You So Adorable?　　Col CB-469, DO-783
　NOTE: The identity of the vocalist of matrix CA-12692 is not known.
With ROY FOX AND HIS BAND.　　London, May 19, 1932.
GB-4489-2　You've Got What Gets Me　　Dec F-3014
GB-4490-3　I Got Rhythm　　—
GB-4491-2　Put That Sun Back In The Sky　　Dec F-3015
GB-4492-1, -2　The Echo Of A Song　　Rejected
With THE NEW MAYFAIR ORCHESTRA, directed by Ray Noble.
　　　　London, May 27, 1932.
OB-2892-2　Songs Everybody Is Singing—Part 1　HMV B-4208
　　　(Al Bowlly sings a chorus of 'By The Fireside')
OB-2893-2　Songs Everybody Is Singing—Part 2　HMV B-4208
　　　(Al Bowlly sings a chorus of 'What Makes You So Adorable?')
　NOTE: Matrix 2B-2891 has no vocal refrain.
With ARTHUR LALLY AND HIS ORCHESTRA (Decca F-3006, F-3067) or BUDDY
LEWIS AND HIS ORCHESTRA (Panachord 25240) or JACK HOLMES AND HIS
ORCHESTRA (Mayfair G-2170).　　London, June 1, 1932.
GB-4537-2　A Hiking Holiday With Bert Feldman　Dec F-3006
　　　　—Part 1 (Al Bowlly sings a chorus of 'Was That The Human
　　　　Thing To Do?')
GB-4538-1　A Hiking Holiday With Bert Feldman　Dec F-3006
　　　　—Part 2 (Al Bowlly sings a chorus of 'When The Rest Of The
　　　　Crowd Goes Home')
PB-1008-2　Good Evening　　Dec F-3067, M-1195,
　　　　　　　　　　　　　　Pana 25240, May G-2170
　　　　　　　　　　　　　　Pan
PB-1009-2　My Sunny Monterey　　—　—
With RAY NOBLE AND THE NEW MAYFAIR DANCE ORCHESTRA.
　　　　London, June 8, 1932.
OB-3094-3　Good Evening　　HMV B-6193, EA-1119
OB-3095-2　The Echo Of A Song　　—
OB-3096-2　Dreams That Don't Grow Old　　HMV B-6192
With ROY FOX AND HIS BAND.　　London, June 10, 1932.
GB-4492-3　The Echo Of A Song　　Dec F-3015, Br 6457
GB-4559-2　It's Always Goodbye　　Dec F-3028
GB-4560-3　Lullaby Of The Leaves　　Dec F-3029
GB-4561-2　Gone Forever　　—
GB-4562-2　What Makes You So Adorable?　　Dec F-3028
With ARTHUR LALLY AND HIS ORCHESTRA,　London, June 30, 1932.
GB-4610-2　Drums In My Heart　　Dec F-3057
GB-4611-1　Ev'ry Day's A Lucky Day　　—　M-1175
136

With the SAVOY HOTEL ORPHEANS.　　London, July 18, 1932.
CA-12892-2　I Heard　　　　　　　Col CB-483, DO-805
CA-12893-1　What A Life!　　　　　Col CB-482　　—
CA-12894-2　A Great Big Bunch Of You　　—　　DO-806

With ROY FOX AND HIS BAND.　　London, July 20, 1932.
GB-4679-3　Minnie The Moocher's Wedding Day　Dec F-3063
GB-4680-3　Roy Fox's Commentary on Minnie The　—
　　　　　　Moocher's Wedding (Speech in Chinese (?) by Al Bowlly)
GB-4681-2　One More Affair　　　　Dec F-3093
GB-4682-1, -2　Marta　　　　　　　Rejected

With RAY NOBLE AND THE NEW MAYFAIR DANCE ORCHESTRA.
　　　　　　　　　　　　　　　　London, July 20, 1932.
OB-2367-2　Why Be So Unkind To Me?　HMV B-6220, EA-1143
OB-2368-1　Please Don't Mention It (with Anona　HMV B-6129　—
　　　　　　Winn)
OB-2369-2　Where Are You? (Girl Of My　HMV B-6220
　　　　　　Dreams) (with Anona Winn)
OB-2370-2　Pagan Moon　　　　　　HMV B-6219

With ARTHUR LALLY AND HIS ORCHESTRA.　London, July 23, 1932.
GB-4689-1　We've Got The Moon And Sixpence　Dec F-3066*
GB-4690-2　Is I In Love? I Is　　　　　　—　　*

Acc. by small instrumental group.　　London, July 26, 1932.
GB-4696-1　Please Don't Mention It　　Dec F-3128, M-422,
　　　　　　　　　　　　　　　　　　　　　　　　　M-1203
GB-4697-2　Wherever You Are　　　　—　　　　—　—

With ROY FOX AND HIS BAND.　　London, August 8, 1932.
GB-4682-4　Marta　　　　　　　　　Dec F-3093
GB-4715-1　Wherever You Are　　　Dec F-3094
GB-4716-2　Just Another Dream Of You　—
GB-4717-1　Ooh! That Kiss!　　　　Dec F-3099
GB-4718-2　You're My Everything　　—

With RAY NOBLE AND THE NEW MAYFAIR DANCE ORCHESTRA.
　　　　　　　　　　　　　　　　London, September 1, 1932.
OB-3182-2　Looking On The Bright Side Of Life　HMV B-4237, Vic 24212
OB-3183-2　The Younger Generation　　　　　HMV B-2638, Vic 25020
OB-3185-1　You're More Than All The World　HMV B-6237
　　　　　　To Me
　　NOTE: Matrix OB-3184 has no vocal refrain.

Acc. by small instrumental group.　　London, September 7, 1932.
GB-4842-3　Happy-Go-Lucky You (And Broken-　Dec F-3145
　　　　　　Hearted Me)
GB-4843-1　It Was So Beautiful　　　　—

With RAY NOBLE AND THE NEW MAYFAIR DANCE ORCHESTRA.
London, September 8, 1932.
OB-3195-2 I'll Do My Best To Make You Happy HMV B-6245, Vic 24333
OB-3196-2 Love Is The Sweetest Thing — —
NOTE: The vocalist on matrices OB-3197/8 is John Henry.

With ROY FOX AND HIS BAND. London, September 9, 1932.
GB-4866-3 The Night When Love Was Born Dec F-3152
GB-4867-1 Are You Prepared (To Be True?) —
GB-4868-1 If You Were Only Mine Dec F-3151
GB-4869-2 Call It A Day —

Acc. by orchestra. London, September 19, 1932.
GB-4901-1, -2, -3 Love Is The Sweetest Thing Dec Rejected
GB-4902-1, -2 I'll Do My Best To Make You Happy —

With ARTHUR LALLY AND HIS ORCHESTRA. London, September 21, 1932.
GB-4919-2 Dance Of The Cuckoos Dec F-3186
GB-4921-1 This Is My Love Song Pana 25303, May G-2203
NOTE: Mayfair as JACK HOLMES AND HIS ORCHESTRA. Matrix GB-4920 is by Roy Henderson, apparently without connection with the Arthur Lally session.

With ROY FOX AND HIS BAND. London, September 23, 1932.
GB-4936-2 The Old Man Of The Mountain Dec F-3181
GB-4937-3 How'm I Doin'? (Hey-Hey) (Vocal Dec F-3198
    refrain by Nat Gonella and chorus including Al Bowlly)
GB-4938-2 Moon Dec F-3198
GB-4939-3 All Of A Sudden Dec F-3181

With ARTHUR LALLY AND HIS ORCHESTRA. London, September 29, 1932.
GB-4957-1 Hello Mike Dec F-3187
GB-4958-2 Considerin' — May G-2202
GB-4959-3 Looking On The Bright Side Pana 25303*
    May G-2203
GB-4960-2 Wicked Mr. Punch Dec F-3186
NOTE: Mayfair as JACK HOLMES AND HIS ORCHESTRA; Decca F-3186 as RUDY STARITA—Xylophone Solo with Orchestra.

Acc. by orchestra. London, October 7, 1932.
GB-4901-6 Love Is The Sweetest Thing Dec F-3194
GB-4902-3 I'll Do My Best To Make You Happy —
GB-4994-1 My Romance Dec F-3218
GB-4995-1 Keep Your Last Goodnight For Me —

With RAY NOBLE AND THE NEW MAYFAIR DANCE ORCHESTRA.
London, October 11, 1932.
OB-4069-1 Don't Say Goodbye HMV B-6251
OB-4070-2 Song Of The Bells HMV B-6249

OB-4071-1	A Bedtime Story	HMV B-6250, EA-1223, Vic 24226
OB-4072-2	Marching Along Together	HMV B-6249
OB-4073-2	You, Just You	HMV B-6251
OB-4074-3	Rock Your Cares Away	HMV B-6250, Vic 24302, 25262

With LEW STONE AND THE MONSEIGNEUR BAND. Matrix GA-5065 features the band and Al Bowlly, and various other Decca artists.

London, October 21, 1932.

GB-5058-1, -2, -3	Nightfall	Rejected
GB-5059-1, -2, -3	Rain, Rain, Go Away	–
GB-5060-1, -2	In The Still Of The Night	Rejected
GB-5061-1, -2	Why Waste Your Tears?	–
GA-5065-2	O. K. Decca—Part 2 (Al Bowlly sings a chorus of 'Happy-Go-Lucky You And Broken-Hearted Me')	Dec K-684

London, October 31, 1932.

GB-5058-5	Nightfall	Dec F-3234
GB-5059-5	Rain, Rain, Go Away	Dec F-3233
GB-5060-5	In The Still Of The Night	Dec F-3234
GB-5061-1	Why Waste Your Tears?	Dec F-3233

London, November 11, 1932.

GB-5158-1, -2	I Can't Write The Words	Dec rejected
GB-5159-1, -2	Let's Put Out The Lights And Go To Sleep (with Mary Charles)	–

Acc. by orchestra directed by George Scott-Wood (on Decca F-3275) or by George Scott-Wood (pno.) (on Decca F-3304). Matrices GB-5174/5 are by other artists entirely.

London, November 15, 1932

GB-5172-3	So Ashamed	Dec F-3275
GB-1573-1	Rosa Mia	–
GB-5176-1	I'll Follow You	Dec F-3304
GB-5177-3	A Million Dreams	–

With LEW STONE AND THE MONSEIGNEUR BAND.

London, November 16, 1932.

GB-5158-5	I Can't Write The Words	Dec F-3270*
GB-5159-4	Let's Put Out The Lights (And Go To Sleep) (with Mary Charles)	– *

London, November 29, 1932.

GB-5261-2	Junk Man Blues (with chorus)	Dec F-3313*
GB-5261-2	Balloons	Dec F-3314*
GB-5263-2	My Woman	Dec F-3313*

NOTE: Matrix GB-5264 was scheduled to be made at this session, but the allotted time expired before it could be recorded.

		London, December 2, 1932.
GB-5264-2	I'll Never Be The Same	Dec F-3314*
GB-5280-3	You'll Always Be The Same Sweetheart To Me	Dec F-3345*

With RAY NOBLE AND HIS ORCHESTRA.   London, December 8, 1932.
OB-4356-2	Here Lies Love	HMV B-6283
OB-4357-1	Please	– El EG-2778
OB-4358-3	Brighter Than The Sun	HMV B-6302, Vic 24314

With LEW STONE AND THE MONSEIGNEUR BAND.
London, December 9, 1932.
GB-5314-2, -3	The Girl Who Thought... Part 1	Dec F-3324
GB-5315-1	The Girl Who Thought...—Part 2	–
GB-5316-1	Let's All Sing Like The Birdies Sing	Dec F-3345

With RAY NOBLE AND HIS ORCHESTRA.   London, December 14, 1932.
| OB-4365-1 | What More Can I Ask? | HMV B-6302, Vic 24314 |

NOTE: Al Bowlly does not sing on other titles from this session.

Acc. by George Scott-Wood (pno.)   London, December 21, 1932.
| KB-216-2 | Glorious Devon | Dec F-3369 |

With LEW STONE AND THE MONSEIGNEUR BAND.
London, December 23, 1932.
GB-5398-1	What More Can I Ask?	Dec F-3373*
GB-5399-1	Brighter Than The Sun	– *
GB-5400-1	Ich Liebe Dich, My Dear	Dec F-3372*
GB-5401-2	Lying In The Hay	–

London, January 10, 1933.
| GB-5445-2 | Little Nell (Al Bowlly speaks the part of the villain) | Dec F-3394 |
| GB-5446-1 | A Letter To My Mother (A Brivele der Mame) (In Yiddish) | Dec F-3428 |

NOTE: Al Bowlly does not sing on other titles from this session.

With RAY NOBLE AND HIS ORCHESTRA.   London, January 12, 1933.
OB-4394-2	A Little Street Where Old Friends Meet	HMV B-6305
OB-4395-2	Lying In The Hay	HMV B-6306, EA-1187, El EG-2748, Vic 24297
OB-4396-1	Wanderer	HMV B-6306, EA-1198, El EG-2748, Vic 24297
OB-4397-1	Just An Echo In The Valley	HMV B-6305

With LEW STONE AND THE MONSEIGNEUR BAND.
London, January 27, 1933.
| GB-5446-4 | A Letter To My Mother (A Brivele der Mame) (In Yiddish) | Dec F-3428 |

GB-5521-2	What More Can I Ask?	Dec F-3459*, Br 6576
GB-5522-2	In Santa Lucia	Dec F-3456
GB-5523-1	Please Handle With Care	–
GB-5524-1	The World Is So Small	Dec F-3455
GB-5525-1	Mediterranean Madness	– 656

With RAY NOBLE AND HIS ORCHESTRA. London, January 31, 1933.

OB-6414-1	Butterflies In The Rain	HMV B-6316, EA-1236, Vic 24296
OB-6415-1	A Letter To My Mother	HMV B-6317, Vic 24308
OB-6416-1	Play, Fiddle, Play	HMV B-6318, El EG-3402

NOTE: Last side as NEW MAYFAIR DANCE ORCHESTRA.

The next session is entered in the HMV files as by 'Mr. Blunt and his Orchestra', evidently Jack Jackson's Orchestra, but there is no indication that Al Bowlly is the vocalist, although this is quite likely.

London, February 1, 1933.

OB-6421-1, -2	Come On, Be Happy	HMV rejected
OB-6422-1, -2	One Little Word Led To Another	–

With RAY NOBLE AND HIS ORCHESTRA. London, February 7, 1933.

OB-6320-1	Look What You've Done	HMV B-6321, K-6907
OB-6431-2	Standing On The Corner	HMV B-6317, Vic 24308
OB-6432-2	Poor Me, Poor You	HMV B-6318, El EG-2390
OB-6433-1	Have You Ever Been Lonely?	HMV B-6319, Vic 24278
OB-6434-1	Wheezy Anna	HMV B-6316, Vic 24287
OB-6435-2	Love Tales	HMV B-6319, Vic 24278

NOTE: HMV B-6318 as NEW MAYFAIR DANCE ORCHESTRA. The divergence between the first matrix number and the others is caused by its having been made in a different studio.

With THE NEW MAYFAIR DANCE ORCHESTRA, directed by Ray Noble (a different band from Ray Noble's regular group). London, February 20, 1933.

OB-6440-1	Can't We Meet Again?	HMV B-6320
OB-6441-2	Sweetheart	–

NOTE: Matrices OB-6442/4 inclusive have no vocal refrains.

With JOHN JACKSON (Jack Jackson) AND HIS ORCHESTRA.

London, February 24, 1933.

OB-6421-4	Come On, Be Happy	HMV B-6330
OB-6449-2	Let Bygones Be Bygones	–
OB-6450-2	I'm Playing With Fire	HMV B-6322
OB-6451-1	Sittin' In The Dark	– EA-1202

With RAY NOBLE AND HIS ORCHESTRA. London, February 27, 1933.

OB-6452-1	The Moment I Saw You	HMV B-6325, Vic 24610, 25313, 120859 (Canadian)

OB–6453–1 My Heart's To Let   HMV B–6323, Vic 24341
OB–6454–1 When You've Fallen In Love   –   –
NOTE: Al Bowlly does not sing on matrix OB–6455.

With LEW STONE AND THE MONSEIGNEUR BAND.
                                    London, March 2, 1933.
GB–5613–2 My Heart's To Let   Dec F–3496
GB–5614–2 When You've Fallen In Love   –
GB–5625–1 Someone To Care For   Dec F–3502
GB–5626–2 Won't You Stay To Tea?   –
NOTE: Matrices GB–5615/24 inclusive are by other artists on other dates.

With RAY NOBLE AND HIS ORCHESTRA.   London, March 16, 1933.
OB–6474–1 Three Wishes   HMV B–6332, Vic 24347
OB–6476–2 Let Me Give My Happiness To You   –   –
OB–6478–2 Hustlin' And Bustlin' For Baby   HMV B–6331
OB–6479–1 Stay On The Right Side Of The Road   –   Vic 24375
NOTE: Matrices OB–6475 and OB–6477 are non-vocal versions of the titles on OB–6474 and OB–6476 respectively.
                                    London, March 17, 1933.
OB–6357–1, –2 Brother, Can You Spare A Dime? HMV test
OB–6358–1, –2 Sweetheart   –

With THE SCOTT-WOOD ACCORDION QUARTET.
                                    London, c April 3, 1933.
CE–4949–1 Sweetheart   Par R–1476
CE–4950–1 Can't We Meet Again?   Par R–1506, A–3628
CE–4952–1 The Goodnight Waltz   –   –
CE–4953–1 Oh! Mr. Moon   Par R–1476
NOTE: Al Bowlly does not appear to sing on matrix CE–4951.

With LEW STONE AND THE MONSEIGNEUR BAND.
                                    London, April 5, 1933.
GB–5727–2 Oh! Mr. Moon   Dec F–3535
GB–5728–1 Three Wishes   Dec F–3534
GB–5729–1 Let Me Give My Happiness To You   –
GB–5730–1 And So I Married The Girl   Dec F–3535

With THE NEW MAYFAIR ORCHESTRA, directed by Clifford Greenwood.
                                    London, April 6, 1933.
2B–6493–1 Venetian Nights   HMV C–2565
          (Al Bowlly sings part of the 'Barcarolle' from Offenbach's 'Tales Of Hoffman' with Suzanne Botterill)

Acc. by small instrumental group.   London, April 20, 1933.
GB–5769–2 Maria, My Own   Dec F–3560
GB–5770–2 That's All That Matters To Me   –
GB–5771–1 You Must Believe Me   Dec F–3547
GB–5772–2 Goodnight But Not Goodbye   –

With RAY NOBLE AND HIS ORCHESTRA.   London, April 25, 1933.
OB-6515-3 I'm One Of The Lads Of Valencia   HMV B-6344
           (with Ray Noble and chorus)
OB-6516-1 The Village Band (with Ray Noble   –
           and chorus)
OB-6517-1 Dinah   HMV test for Ray Noble
                                    London, May 3, 1933.
OB-6527-1 Waltzing In A Dream   HMV B-6348, EA-1226
OB-6528-2 Maybe I Love You Too Much   HMV B-6347
OB-6529-2 It's Within Your Power   –
                                    London, May 10, 1933.
OB-6533-2 The Old Spinning-Wheel   HMV B-6348,
                                              El EG-3083, Vic 24357
OB-6534-2 When My Little Pomeranian Met   HMV B-6358
           Your Little Pekinese (with Frances Day)
OB-6535-1 That's What Life Is Made Of   HMV B-6361,
                                              El EG-2836, Vic 24599
   NOTE: The vocalist on matrices OB-6537/8 is Ace Roland.
With RAY NOBLE AND HIS ORCHESTRA.   London, May 16, 1933.
OB-6549-1 Hiawatha's Lullaby   HMV B-6359, EA-1226
OB-6550-1, -2 For You Alone   Rejected
OB-6551-4 I Shall Still Keep Smiling Along   HMV B-6359, EA-1236,
                                              Vic 24393
                                    London, May 24, 1933.
OB-6560-3 All Over Italy (with chorus)   HMV B-6364
OB-6561-1 Seven Years With The Wrong Woman   Vic 24388
With LEW STONE AND THE MONSEIGNEUR BAND.
                                    London, June 7, 1933.
GB-5958-2 I Lay Me Down To Sleep   Dec F-3603
GB-5960-1 In The Park In Paree   Dec F-3592
GB-5961-1 The Language Of Love   Dec F-3603
   NOTE: Despite the label, matrix GB-5959 has no vocal refrain.
With RAY NOBLE AND HIS ORCHESTRA.   London, June 16, 1933.
OB-6593-2 You're Mine, You   HMV B-6370, EA-1240
OB-6594-2 Gypsy Fiddles   HMV B-6367
OB-6595-2 Something Came And Got Me In   HMV B-6369
           The Spring
   NOTE: HMV B-6369 as NEW MAYFAIR DANCE ORCHESTRA.
                                    London, June 20, 1933.
OB-6597-2 A Couple Of Fools In Love   HMV B-6366
OB-6598-2 I Only Want One Girl   –
   NOTE: Matrices OB-6599 and OB-6600 have no vocal refrains.
                                    London, July 5, 1933.
OB-5012-2 The Shadow Waltz   HMV B-6376

OB-5013-1   Pettin' In The Park   HMV B-6375,
                                               El EG-2795
OB-5015-1   I've Got To Sing A Torch-Song   –
NOTE: Matrices OB-5014 and OB-5016 are non-vocal versions of the titles on OB-5013 and OB-5015 respectively.
                              London, July 12, 1933.
OB-4634-2   Roll Up The Carpet   HMV B-6380, EA-1261
                                               Vic 24420, 25262
OB-4635-1   It's Sunday Down In Caroline   HMV B-6381,
                                               El EG-2883
                              London, July 13, 1933.
OB-5028-1   Si Petite   HMV B-6381,
                                               El EG-2883
OB-5029-2   If You'll Say 'Yes', Cherie   HMV B-6379, EA-1261,
                                               El EG-2798
OB-5030-2   There's A Cabin In The Pines   –
OB-5031-1   On The Other Side Of Lovers' Lane HMV B-6380, Vic 24420

With EDDIE POLA AND COMPANY, in the character of 'Bang Horseby'.
                              London, July 25, 1933.
CAX-6900-1 America Calling (A Burlesque on   Col DX-499, DOX-391
            American radio programmes)
            Part 1—Al Bowlly sings a chorus of 'Cuddle Up Close'
CAX-6901-1, -4 2—Al Bowlly sings a chorus of 'You'll Never Understand'
Acc. by unknown viola, pno. and gtr.   London, July 26, 1933.
GB-6056-1   Moonstruck   Dec F-3627
GB-6057-1   There's A Cabin In The Pines   Dec F-3638
GB-6058-1   Learn To Croon   Dec F-3627
GB-6059-2   I'm Gettin' Sentimental Over You   Dec F-3638

With LEW STONE AND THE MONSEIGNEUR BAND.
                              London, August 1, 1933.
TB-1019-2   Isn't It Heavenly?   Dec F-3630
NOTE: Al Bowlly does not sing on other titles from this session.

With LEW STONE AND THE MONSEIGNEUR BAND.
                              London, September 15, 1933.
TB-1068-2   Blue Prelude   Dec F-3675
TB-1069-2   Adorable   Dec F-3676
NOTE: Al Bowlly does not sing on other titles from this session.

With RAY NOBLE AND HIS ORCHESTRA.   London, September 18, 1933.
OB-5084-2   Mademoiselle   HMV B-6394, EA-1274,
                                               Vic 24624
OB-5085-2   How Could We Be Wrong?   HMV B-6396,
                                               El EG-3026, Vic 24872
NOTE: Matrix OB-5086 has no vocal refrain.

                                    London, September 19, 1933.
OB-5091-2 It's Bad For Me   HMV B-6394, EA-1337,
                                       El EG-2950, Vic 24872
OB-5092-2 Trouble In Paradise   HMV B-6394
OB-5093-2 Oh! Johanna   HMV B-6397, EA-1274
OB-5094-1, -2 I've Got To Pass Your House   Rejected
              To Get To My House

   NOTE: HMV B-6397 as NEW MAYFAIR DANCE ORCHESTRA.

                                    London, October 12, 1933.
OB-4672-1 Snow Ball   HMV B-6408
OB-4673-2 Dinner At Eight   HMV B-6409
OB-4674-1 Experiment   HMV B-6408, EA-1337,
                                     El EG-2950, Vic 25006
OB-5133-1 Weep No More, My Baby   HMV B-6409,
                                     El EG-2919
OB-5134-2 Love Locked Out   HMV B-6407, Vic 24485
OB-5135-1 Happy And Contented (with Eve Becke)   –

   NOTE: The first three titles above were made in a different studio from the last three, hence the large gap in the matrix numbers.

Acc. by orchestra directed by Carroll Gibbons.
                                  London, October 16, 1933.
GB-6196-2 Night And Day   Dec F-3695
GB-6197-2 Love Locked Out   –

With LEW STONE AND THE MONSEIGNEUR BAND.
                                  London, October 18, 1933.
TB-1089-2 From Me To You   Dec F-3716
   NOTE: Al Bowlly does not sing on other titles from this session.
                                  London, October 24, 1933.
TB-1095-1 Don't Change   Dec F-3821, 496
TB-1096-2 The Day You Came Along Dec F-3722
TB-1097-2 Thanks   –
   NOTE: The vocalist on matrix TB-1098 is Nat Gonella.
                                  London, October 25, 1933.
GB-6242-2 The Bands That Matter—Part 1   Dec F-3723
          (Al Bowlly sings a chorus of 'Isn't It Heavenly?')

With RAY NOBLE AND HIS ORCHESTRA. London, October 27, 1933.
OB-4680-2 Goodnight, Little Girl Of My   HMV B-6413, EA-1329,
              Dreams   El EG-2919
OB-4699-1 Thanks   –
OB-4700-2 My Hat's On The Side Of My Head HMV B-6421, Vic 24624

With LEW STONE AND HIS BAND (from this point on until the end of 1934, the band was sub-titled 'At the Monseigneur Restaurant, London'.)

                                    London, November 3, 1933.
GB-6277-1 How Could We Be Wrong?   Dec F-3734
GB-6280-1 Experiment
   NOTE: Matrices GB-6278/9 have no vocal refrains.

With RAY NOBLE AND HIS ORCHESTRA.   London, November 9, 1933.
OB-5181-1 Hand In Hand   HMV B-6423
OB-5182-1 And So Goodbye   HMV B-6422
OB-5183-1 This Is Romance   –

Acc. by unknown orchestra.   London, November 13, 1933.
GB-6317-1 Fancy Our Meeting   Dec F-3742
GB-6318-1 Lover, Come Back To Me   –

With RAY NOBLE AND HIS ORCHESTRA.   London, November 29, 1933.
OB-5200-1 Song Without Words   HMV B-6438, Vic 24555
OB-5801-2 When You Were The Girl On The HMV B-6432, K-7320,
           Scooter (with Elsie Carlisle)   El EG-2971
   NOTE: The vocalist on matrix OB-5199 is Bobbie Comber.

With LEW STONE AND HIS BAND.   London, December 1, 1933.
GB-6380-2 Weep No More, My Baby   Dec F-3783
GB-6381-3 Close Your Eyes   –
GA-6382-1 Lew Stone Favourites—'Ten-Thirty Tuesday Night!'
           Part 1—Al Bowlly sings a chorus of 'Minnie The Moocher.
           (assisted by the band)   Dec K-715
GA-6383-1 Part 2—Al Bowlly sings a chorus of 'Brother, Can You Spare A
           Dime'

With RAY NOBLE AND HIS ORCHESTRA.   London, December 7, 1933.
OB-5821-2 My Song Goes Round The World HMV B-6438, Vic 24555
OB-5822-2 Oceans Of Time   HMV B-6450,
                                        El EG-3083, Vic 24603
OB-5823-1 Close Your Eyes   HMV B-6441,
                                        El EG-2970
                                     London, December 20, 1933.
OB-5833-1 On A Steamer Coming Over   HMV B-6440,
                                        El EG-3027, Vic 24575
OB-5834-1 Did You Ever See A Dream Walking? HMV B-6441
OB-5835-2 You Ought To See Sally On Sunday HMV B-6440, Vic 24575
   NOTE:The last title is said to have been issued on Asterisk 955, but we are
   at present uncertain of the nationality of this label, which may be a pirate
   make.

With LEW STONE AND HIS BAND.   London, December 29, 1933.
GB-6441-1 Eadie Was A Lady   Dec F-3825
GB-6442-2 Who'll Buy An Old Gold Ring? Dec F-2842
GB-6443-1 Dark Clouds   Dec F-3826
   NOTE: Al Bowlly does not sing on other titles from this session.

Acc. by small orchestra.　　　　　　London, January 4, 1934.
GB–6457–2　Everything I Have Is Yours　　Dec F–3853
GB–6458–2　That's Me Without You　　　　–
With LEW STONE AND HIS BAND.　　London, January 9, 1934.
GB–6474–2　Louisiana Hayride　　　　Dec F–3840
　NOTE: Al Bowlly does not sing on other titles from this session.
With RAY NOBLE AND HIS ORCHESTRA.　London, February 1, 1934.
OB–4768–2　Unless　　　　　　　　HMV B–6453, EA–1441
OB–4769–2　Have A Heart　　　　　HMV B–6459
OB–4770–1, –2　Who Walks In When I Walk Out? HMV B–6453, Vic 24594
　NOTE: The last title is apparently the reverse of OB–5835–2 (see above) on
　　Asterisk 955.
With LEW STONE AND HIS BAND.　　London, February 15, 1934.
GB–6538–1　Faint Harmony　　　　　Dec F–3883
GB–6539–1　Lullaby In Blue　　　　　Dec F–3884
GB–6540–2　Gosh! I Must Be Falling In Love　–
GB–6574–2　Wagon Wheels　　　　　Dec F–3905
GB–6575–1　Coffee In The Morning (Kisses In　–
　　　　　　　The Night)
GB–6576–2　Vamp Till Ready　　　　Dec F–3906
　NOTE: Matrices GB–6541/73 inclusive are by other artists on other dates.
　　On GB–6577, there is no vocal refrain.
With RAY NOBLE AND HIS ORCHESTRA.　London, February 16, 1934.
OB–5899–2　It's Time To Say Goodnight　HMV B–6459, EA–1347,
　　　　　　　　　　　　　　　　　　　El EG–3024
OB–5900–2　Midnight, The Stars And You　HMV B–6461, EA–1338,
　　　　　　　　　　　　　　　　　　　El EG–3023, Vic 24700
OB–5901–1　This Little Piggie Went To Market　HMV B–6461,
　　　　　　　　　　　　　　　　　　　El EG–3024
　　　　　　　　　　　　　　　London, February 21, 1934.
OB–4791–2　Over On The Sunny Side　HMV B–6463, EA–1338,
　　　　　　　　　　　　　　　　　　　El EG–3054
OB–4792–5　Wagon Wheels　　　　　HMV B–6469
　　　　　　　　　　　　　　　　　　　El EG–3048
　NOTE: Al Bowlly does not sing on other titles from this session.
　　　　　　　　　　　　　　　London, March 12, 1934.
OB–5936–1　Not Bad?　　　　　　　HMV B–4671, Vic 24619
OB–5937–1　What Now?　　　　　　HMV B–6470, Vic 24711
With LEW STONE AND HIS BAND.　　London, March 16, 1934.
TB–1133–2　In A Shelter From A Shower　Dec F–3942
　NOTE: Matrices TB–1131 and TB–1132 have no vocal refrains.
　　　　　　　　　　　　　　　London, March 23, 1934.
TB–1158–2　Because It's Love　　　　Dec F–3942

TB-1159-1   It's Psychological   Rejected
TB-1160-1   Mauna Loa   Dec F-3952
    NOTE: The vocalist on matrix TB-1161 is Nat Gonella.

With RAY NOBLE AND HIS ORCHESTRA.   London, April 5, 1934.
OB-6858-2   You Have Taken My Heart   HMV B-6477, EA-1441
OB-6859-2   One Morning In May   HMV B-6478,
                                        El EG-3084
OB-6860-2   You Ought To Be In Pictures HMV B-6477

Acc. by Monia Liter (pno.)   London, April 9, 1934.
GB-6684-2   True   Dec F-3963
GB-6685-2   The Very Thought Of You   –
GB-6686-2   You Oughta Be In Pictures   Dec F-3956
GB-6687-2   Little Dutch Mill   –

With RAY NOBLE AND HIS ORCHESTRA.   London, April 21, 1934.
OB-6872-1   The Old Covered Bridge   HMV B-6484, EA-1371
OB-6873-2   Little Dutch Mill   HMV B-6482, EA-1379,
                                        El EG-3076
OB-6874-1   The Very Thought Of You   – EA-1365,
                                        El EG-6690 –
                                        Vic 24657, 20-2950

With LEW STONE AND HIS BAND.   London, April 24, 1934.
TB-1206-1   You're My Thrill   Dec F-3980
TB-1208-1   Melody In Spring   Dec F-3979
    NOTE: The vocalist on matrix TB-1209 is Joe Ferrie; Matrix TB-1207 has
    no vocal refrain at all.
                                     London, April 25, 1934.
TB-1212-2   What Is There To Take Its Place? Dec F-5003
TB-1214-1   Lonely Feet   Dec F-3985
TB-1215-2   Ending With A Kiss   Dec F-3979
    NOTE: Matrix TB-1213 has no vocal refrain.

With RAY NOBLE AND HIS ORCHESTRA.   London, April 27, 1934.
OB-5981-2   She Loves Me Not   HMV B-6485
OB-5982-2   After All, You're All I'm After –
OB-5983-2   My Sweet   HMV B-6484, Vic 25232

With LEW STONE AND HIS BAND.   London, May 3, 1934.
TB-1228-2   Hand In Hand   Dec F-3985
TB-1229-2   Riding On A Hay Cart Home   Dec F-5004
TB-1230-2   I Love You Truly   Dec F-5003

With THE BOHEMIANS, directed by Walter Goehr.
                                     London, c May 11, 1934.
CAX-7131-1 Wonder Bar—Film Selection   Col DX-583, DOX-428
            Part 1—Al Bowlly sings a chorus of 'Wonder Bar' and
            'Goin' To Heaven On A Mule'

148

CAX-7132-1	Part 2—Al Bowlly sings a chorus of 'Don't Say Goodnight, and the reprise of 'Wonder Bar'	

With RAY NOBLE AND HIS ORCHESTRA. London, May 31, 1934.
OB-6956-2	The Show Is Over	HMV B-6492
OB-6957-1	I Love You Truly	- K-7320, Vic 24806
OB-6958-2	Little Man, You've Had A Busy Day	HMV B-6491, El EG-3103
OB-6959-1	Beat O' My Heart	- EA-1377 -
OB-6960-4	Night On The Desert	HMV B-6496, EA-1379

NOTE: Matrix OB-6961 has no vocal refrain.

With LEW STONE AND HIS BAND. London, June 15, 1934.
TB-1311-2	Riptide	Dec F-5017
TB-1312-2	Night On The Desert	-
TB-1313-1	Beat O' My Heart	Dec F-5018*
TB-1314-2	Easy Come—Easy Go	- *

With RAY NOBLE AND HIS ORCHESTRA. London, June 28, 1934.
OB-7428-2	I'll String Along With You	HMV B-6503
OB-7429-2	Fair And Warmer	-
OB-7430-1	Hold My Hand	HMV B-6499

NOTE: The vocalist on matrix OB-7431 is Dorothy Carless.

London, July 2, 1934.
OB-7432-3	Over My Shoulder	HMV B-6504, El EG-3309, Vic 24720
OB-7433-2	When You've Got A Little Springtime	- - -
OB-7434-1, -2	Sweetheart Darlin'	Rejected

London, July 6, 1934.
OB-7435-3	Remember Me	HMV B-6508, EA-1394, El EG-3118
OB-7436-1	Moon Country	HMV B-6507, EA-1440, El EG-3127
OB-7437-1	Happy	- EA-1394 -

London, July 11, 1934.
OB-7441-2	It's All Forgotten Now	HMV B-6509, El EG-3109, Vic 24724
OB-7442-1	All I Do Is Dream Of You	HMV B-6508, El EG-3118
OB-7443-2	Dreamy Serenade	HMV B-6510, EA-1396

Acc. by Monia Liter (pno.) London, July 16, 1934.
TB-1394-1	Madonna Mine	Dec F-5121
TB-1395-1	It's All Forgotten Now	-

With RAY NOBLE AND HIS ORCHESTRA. London, July 18, 1934.
OB-7448-2	I Never Had A Chance	HMV B-6509, EA-1396, El EG-3109

F

OB–7449–2 Lady Of Madrid   HMV B–6510, Vic 24724
OB–7450–2 Little Valley In The Mountains   HMV B–6512,
                                              El EG–3169
OB–7451–1 Driftin' Tide   HMV B–6511, Vic 25006
With LEW STONE AND HIS BAND.   London, July 25, 1924.
TB–1420–2 I Never Had A Chance   Dec F–5131
TB–1421–2 Fare Thee Well   Dec F–5130
   NOTE: The vocalist on matrix TB–1422 is Nat Gonella.
                                        London, August 1, 1934.
TB–1440–2 With My Eyes Wide Open I'm   Dec F–5172
              Dreaming
TB–1441–2 Rolling Home   –
   NOTE: The vocalist on matrices TB–1436/7, also made at this session, is the
   bass player, Tiny Winters.
                                        London, August 3, 1934.
TB–1434–1 As Long As I Live   Dec F–5132
TB–1435–1 I've Had My Moments   Dec F–5131
TB–1449–1 Straight From The Shoulder   Dec F–5158
TB–1450–1 Looking For A Little Bit Of Blue Dec F–5270
TB–1451–2 What A Little Moonlight Can Do   –   444
TB–1452–1 Love In Bloom   Dec F–5158
   NOTE: The vocalist on matrices TB–1448 and TB–1453, also made at this
   session, is Nat Gonella. Matrices TB–1438/9 and TB–1442/7 inclusive are all
   by other artists on other dates. Evidently some of them were allocated prior
   to the actual recording, which for some reason did not take place until some
   time later.
Acc. by Monia Liter (pno.)   London, August 21, 1934.
TB–1495–2 Isle of Capri   Dec F–5188, Ch 40032
TB–1496–2 Judy   –   –
With RAY NOBLE AND HIS ORCHESTRA.   London, August 24, 1934.
OEA–803–2 The Prize Waltz   HMV B–6516
OEA–805–2 Grinzing   HMV B–6519, Vic 24771
OEA–806–2 Freckle Face, You're Beautiful   HMV B–6512, EA–1425
   NOTE: Matrix OEA–804 has no vocal refrain.
                                        London, August 30, 1934.
OEA–816–2 Isle Of Capri   HMV B–6519, EA–1425,
                                              Vic 24771
OEA–817–1 Love, Wonderful Love   HMV B–6514
OEA–818–2 Dreaming A Dream   HMV B–6520,
                                              El EG–3196, Vic 24850
Acc. by orchestra, directed by Victor Young.
                                        New York, October 30, 1934.
38923–A If I Had A Million Dollars   Dec 293, F–5326
38924–A Be Still, My Heart   –   –

150

With VICTOR YOUNG AND HIS ORCHESTRA. New York, November 2, 1934.
38948-A Say When   Dec 278*
38949-A When Love Comes Swingin' Along   -   *

Acc. by orchestra, directed by Ray Noble. New York, January 12, 1934.
87357-1 You And The Night And The Music   Vic 24855,
                                           HMV EA-1485, N-4378
78358-1, -2 Blue Moon   Vic 24849
87359-1 In A Blue And Pensive Mood   -   HMV B-8302,
                                           BD-230
87360-1 A Little White Gardinea   Vic 24855 - EA-1485 -

With RAY NOBLE AND HIS ORCHESTRA.   New York, February 9, 1935.
87496-1 Soon   Vic 24879*,
                                           HMV BD-140*,
                                           EA-1512
87497-1 Clouds   Vic 24865*,
                                           HMV BD-147*,
                                           EA-1497*, El EG-3323
87498-1 Down By The River   Vic 24879*,
                                           HMV BD-140*,
                                           EA-1512*

With RAY NOBLE AND HIS ORCHESTRA.   New York, March 9, 1935.
89301-1, -2 Flowers For Madame   Vic 24865*,
                                           HMV BD-213*,
                                           EA-1497*, El EG-3323
   NOTE: The other titles for this session have no vocal refrains.

Acc. by orchestra, directed by Ray Noble. New York, March 15, 1935.
893227-1 My Melancholy Baby   Vic 25007, HMV B-8330,
                                           BD-228, EA-1522
89328-1 Everything's Been Done Before   Vic 25004,
                                           HMV BD-226, EA-1506
89329-1 You Opened My Eyes   - HMV B-8330,
                                              BD-228 -
89330-1, -2 Basin Street Blues   Vic 25007,
                                           HMV BD-226, EA-1522

With RAY NOBLE AND HIS ORCHESTRA.   New York, May 10, 1935.
88963-2 Paris In Spring   Vic 25040*,
                                           HMV BD-192*,
                                           EA-1538*, El EG-3412
88964-2 Bon Jour, Mam'selle   As above
   NOTE: Matrices 88965/6 have no vocal refrains.

		New York, June 8, 1935.
92229-1	Top Hat (with The Freshmen)	Vic 25094*,
		HMV BD-247*,
		NE-239*, El EG-3488

NOTE: Matrix 92230 has a vocal refrain by The Freshmen.

		New York, June 10, 1935.
92231-1	The Piccolino	Vic 25094*,
		HMV BD-247*,
		NE-239*, E. EG-2488
92232-1	St. Louis Blues	Vic 25082*,
		HMV BD-5004*

		New York, July 20, 1935.
92747-1	Why Dream?	Vic 25104*
		HMV BD-210*,
		EA-1591*, El EG-3489
92749-1	Why Stars Come Out At Night	Vic 25105*,
		HMV BD-210*,
		El EG-3489
92750-1	I Wished On The Moon	Vic 25104*,
		HMV BD-211*,
		EA-1591*

NOTE: Matrix 92748 has a vocal refrain by The Freshmen.

Acc. by orchestra, directed by Ray Noble. New York, September 18, 1935.

95042-1	Roll Along, Prairie Moon	Vic 25142,
		HMV BD-295, EA-1578
95043-1	Red Sails In The Sunset	— — —

With RAY NOBLE AND HIS ORCHESTRA. New York, November 14, 1935.

98064-1	I'm The Fellow Who Loves You (with The Freshmen)	Vic 25190*
98065-1	Where Am I?	Vic 25187*,
		HMV BD-5072*,
		EA-1625*
98066-1	Dinner For One, Please James	Vic 25187*,
		HMV EA-1625*

		New York, December 9, 1935.
98359-1	With All My Heart	Vic 25209*,
		HMV BD-5028*,
		EA-1644*
98360-1	I Built A Dream One Day	Vic 25200*
98361-1	Somebody Ought To Be Told	— *
98362-1	A Beautiful Lady In Blue	Vic 25209*,
		HMV EA-1644*

		New York, January 23, 1936.
98670-1	Let Yourself Go (with The Freshmen)	Vic 25241★, HMV BD-5047★, EA-1670★
98672-1	Let's Face The Music And Dance	As above, plus El EG-3650★
98673-1	If You Love Me	Vic 25240★, HMV BD-5046★, EA-1674★

NOTE: Matrix 98671 has a vocal refrain by The Freshmen.

With RAY NOBLE AND HIS ORCHESTRA.   New York, March 19, 1936.

99900-1	Yours Truly Is Truly Yours	Vic 25277★, HMV EA-1703★
99901-1	Moonlight In Hilo	Vic 25282★
99902-1	The Touch Of Your Lips	Vic 25277★, HMV EA-1703★
99903-1	Blazin' The Trail	Vic 25282★, HMV BD-5072★, El EG-3853★

New York, May 25, 1936.

101863-1	Empty Saddles	Vic 25346★, HMV BD-5095★, EA-1777★
101864-1	Big Chief De Sota (with Sterling Bose)	Vic 25346★, HMV BD-5095★, El EG-3853★
101865-1	But Definitely	Vic 25336★, HMV BD-5091★
101866-1	When I'm With You	— —

With RAY NOBLE AND HIS ORCHESTRA.   London, August 24, 1936.

2EA-3847-1	Ray Noble Medley	HMV C-2872★, Vic 36194★
	Part 1—Al Bowlly sings a chorus of 'The Touch Of Your Lips'	
2EA-3848-1	Part 2—Al Bowlly sings a chorus of 'Goodnight, Sweetheart'	

With RAY NOBLE AND HIS ORCHESTRA.   New York, September 25, 1936.

0744-1	Easy To Love	Vic 25422★, HMV BD-5147★, EA-1829★, El EG-3838★
0745-1	I've Got You Under My Skin	As above
0746-1	Let's Call A Heart A Heart	Vic 25428★, El EG-3823★
0747-1	One, Two, Button Your Shoe	— —

New York, October 16, 1936.

| 02159-1 | Now | Vic 25448★, |

02160-1	Little Old Lady	HMV BD-5287★, El EG-6242★ As above, plus HMV EA-2017★
02161-1	There's Something In The Air	Vic 25459★, HMV BD-5153★, EA-1840★, El EG-3879★
0262-1	Where The Lazy River Goes By	As above

Acc. by orchestra. London, June 19, 1937.

OEA-5035-1	Carelessly	HMV BD-434, EA-2011
OEA-5036-1	On A Little Dream Ranch	–

London, July 5, 1937.

OEA-5048-1	Blue Hawaii	HMV BD-440
OEA-5049-1	Sweet Is The Word For You	–

With RONNIE MUNRO AND HIS ORCHESTRA. London, July 17, 1937.

OEA-5060-2	Le Touquet	HMV BD-5242★
OEA-5061-1	Vieni, Vieni	– EA-2044★, Vic 25668★
OEA-5062-2	Smile When You Say Goodbye	HMV BD-5248
OEA-5063-2	Hometown	HMV EA-2005, BB B-7334

With AL BOWLLY AND HIS ORCHESTRA (studio group)
New York, December 3, 1937.

017457-1	I Can Dream, Can't I?	BB B-7332, HMV BD-5363, El EG-6397
017458-1	Half Moon On The Hudson	BB B-7317, HMV BD-5363, El EG-6397, RZ G-23368
017459-1	Every Day's A Holiday	BB B-7319, RZ G-23409
017460-1	Sweet As A Song	BB B-7317, RZ G-23368
017461-1	Outside Of Paradise	BB B-7319
017462-1	Sweet Stranger	BB B-7332

With MAURICE WINNICK AND HIS ORCHESTRA.
London, December 29, 1937.

DTB-3472-1	Bei mir bist du schoen	Dec F-6591
DTB-3473-1	There's A Gold-Mine In The Sky	Dec F-6590★
DTB-3474-1	Kiss Me Goodnight	Dec F-6591★

NOTE: Al Bowlly is not a member of the trio that sings on matrix DTB-3471.

Acc. by orchestra. London, January 4, 1938.

OEA-5953-2	Bei mir bist du schoen	HMV BD-493, EA-2087
OEA-5954-1	Marie	– –

With SIDNEY LIPTON AND HIS ORCHESTRA. London, January 13, 1938.
DTB-3495-1 The Lonesome Trail Ain't Lone-   Dec F-6608★ +
            some Any More
DTB-3496-2 It's A Long, Long Way To Your Heart   —   ★
DTB-3497-1 Souvenir Of Love   Dec F-6653★
DTB-3498-1 Trusting My Luck   —   ★

With THE NEW MAYFAIR ORCHESTRA.   London, January 14, 1938.
OEA-5983-1 Rosalie—Selection   HMV BD-502★
           Part 1—Al Bowlly sings a chorus of 'Rosalie'
OEA-5984-1 Part 2—Al Bowlly sings a chorus of 'In The Still Of The
           Night'

With MAURICE WINNICK AND HIS ORCHESTRA.
                                   London, January 20, 1938.
DTB-3509-1 Rosalie   Dec F-6605★
DTB-3510-1 In The Still Of The Night   —   ★
DTB-3511-1 Once In A While   Dec F-6599★
    NOTE: Al Bowlly is not a member of the trio that sings on matrix DTB-3512.

Acc. by orchestra.   London, February 2, 1938.
OEA-5998-2 You're A Sweetheart   HMV BD-503
OEA-5999-2 The Pretty Little Patchwork Quilt —

With LEW STONE AND HIS BAND.   London, February 4, 1938.
DTB-3547-1 I Double Dare You   Dec F-6606★
DTB-3548-2 The Girl In The Alice Blue Gown Dec F-6607★
DTB-3549-1 Little Drummer Boy   —   ★
DTB-3550-2 You're A Sweetheart   Dec F-6606★

With MANTOVANI AND HIS ORCHESTRA. London, March 4, 1938.
CA-16871-2 Something To Sing About   Col FB-1925
CA-16872-1 In My Little Red Book   —
With LEW STONE AND HIS BAND.   London, March 21, 1938.
DTB-3604-1 Sweet Genevieve   Dec F-6642★
DTB-3605-1 In My Little Red Book   —   ★
DTB-3606-1 Moonlight On The Highway   Dec F-6641★
DTB-3607-1 Have You Ever Been In Heaven?   —   ★

With his Crooners Choir, acc. by unknown pno.
                                   London, April 1, 1938.
OEA-6192-1 Sweet As A Song   HMV BD-543
OEA-6193-1 Sweet Someone   —

With LEW STONE AND HIS BAND.   London, April 21, 1938.
DTB-3634-1 By An Old Pagoda   Dec F-6663★
DTB-3635-2 Mama, I Wanna Make Rhythm   Dec F-6664★
DTB-3636-1 In Santa Margherite   Dec F-6663★, X-1556

DTB-3637-1 Ti-Pi-Tin   Dec F-6664★
   NOTE: Decca X-1556 as THE RHYTHM KINGS.
Acc. by George Scott-Wood (pipe-organ). London, May 25, 1938.
OEA-3629-1 Goodnight, Angel   HMV BD-565
OEA-6330-1 When The Organ Played 'Oh,   —
            Promise Me'
OEA-6331-1, -2 Maria, My Own; Marta   Rejected
OEA-6332-1, -2 Stormy Weather; Brother, Can   —
            You Spare A Dime?
With MAURICE WINNICK AND HIS ORCHESTRA.
                                          London, June 13, 1938.
DR-2731-1   When The Organ Played 'Oh,   Dec F-6695★
            Promise Me'
DR-2732-1   Somebody's Thinking Of You Tonight   —
DR-2734-1   My Heaven On Earth   Dec F-6696★
   NOTE: Al Bowlly is not a member of the trio that sings on matrix DR-2733.
With FELIX MENDELSSOHN AND HIS ORCHESTRA.
                                          London, July 1, 1938.
DR-2777-1   The Blackpool Walk   Dec F-6726★
DR-2778-1   The Girl In The Upstairs Flat   —   ★
DR-2779-1   When Granny Wore Her Crinoline   Dec F-6727★, X-1556
DR-2780-1   I'm Saving The Last Waltz For You   —
   NOTE: Decca X-1556 as THE RHYTHM KINGS.
With LEW STONE AND HIS BAND.   London, August 12, 1938.
DR-2839-1   Down And Out Blues (with Sid Colin) Dec F-6743★
DR-2840-1   Little Lady Make-Believe   Dec F-6744★
DR-2841-1   I'm Sorry I Didn't Say I'm Sorry   —   ★
DR-2842-1   You Couldn't Be Cuter   Dec F-6745★
DR-2843-1   Just Let Me Look At You   —   ★
                                          London, August 15, 1938.
DR-2852-1   The Red Maple Leaves   Dec F-6777★
DR-2853-2   Music, Maestro, Please   —   ★
DR-2854-1   I Won't Tell A Soul   Dec F-6763★
DR-2855-1   Say Goodnight To Your Old-   —   ★
            Fashioned Mother
With DON BARRIGO AND HIS HAWAIIAN SWING.
                                          London, August 22, 1938.
CE-2978-1   Star Dust   Par rejected
   NOTE: Al Bowlly does not sing on other titles from this session.
With GERALDO AND HIS ORCHESTRA. London, September 9, 1938.
OEA-6553-2 My Heart Is Taking Lessons   HMV BD-5402
OEA-6554-1 On The Sentimental Side   —
   NOTE: There is no reference to the vocal refrain on either label on this issue.

With LEW STONE AND HIS BAND.　　　London, September 27, 1938.
DR-2927-1　Now It Can Be Told　　　Dec F-6795*
DR-2928-1　On The Sentimental Side　　 　—　　*

With OSCAR RABIN AND HIS ROMANY BAND (at the Hammersmith Palais de Danse).　　　London, September 28, 1938.
R-2924-1　Proud Of You　　　Rex 9384*
 NOTE: Al Bowlly does not sing on other titles from this session.

With LEW STONE AND HIS BAND.　　　London, October 3, 1938.
DR-2950-2　Everyone Should Have A Sweetheart　Dec F-6811
DR-2952-2　The Frog On The Water-Lily　　Dec F-6812*
 NOTE: Al Bowlly does not sing on other titles from this session. His vocal work on DR-2950-2 is wrongly credited on the label to Sid Colin.

With FELIX MENDELSSOHN AND HIS ORCHESTRA.
　　　　　　　　　　　　　　　London, October 10, 1938.
DR-2982-1　Singers On Parade—Part 2　　Dec F-6831
　　　　(Al Bowlly sings a chorus of 'Little Lady Make-Believe')

With GERALDO AND HIS ORCHESTRA.　　London, October 14, 1938.
OEA-6596-1　In A Little Toy Sail Boat　　HMV BD-5421*
OEA-6597-1　Small Fry　　　　　　　　　—
　　　　　　　　　　　　　　　London, November 11, 1938.
OEA-7071-1　Never Break A Promise　　　HMV BD-4528*,
　　　　　　　　　　　　　　　　　　　　EA-2394*
OEA-7072-1　When Mother Nature Sings Her　HMV BD-5427*,
　　　　　Lullaby　　　　　　　　　　　　El EG-6646*
OEA-7073-1　Penny Serenade　　　　　　　HMV BD-5248*,
　　　　　　　　　　　　　　　　　　　　EA-2225*　—
OEA-7074-1　Heart And Soul　　　　　　　HMV BD-5427*,
　　　　　　　　　　　　　　　　　　　　EA-2248*

Acc. by small 'novelty' group.　　London, November 11, 1938.
DR-3053-1　When Mother Nature Sings Her　Dec F-6877
　　　　　Lullaby
DR-3054-1　There's Rain In My Eyes　　　—
DR-3055-1　Al Bowlly Remembers　　　　Dec F-6916
　　　　　Part 1—'Lover, Come Back To Me'; 'Dancing In The Dark'
DR-3056-1　Part 2—'I'm Gonna Sit Right Down And Write Myself A Letter'; 'Auf Wiedersehen, My Dear'

With LEW STONE AND HIS BAND.　　　London, November 28, 1938.
DR-3119-1　All Ashore　　　　　　　　Dec F-6890*
CR-3120-1　Penny Serenade　　　　　　　—　　*
DR-3121-1　Any Broken Hearts To Mend?　Dec F-6891*
DR-3122-1　Georgia's Gotta Moon　　　　—　　*

157

With GERALDO AND HIS ORCHESTRA. London, December 3, 1938.
OEA-6965-1 Two Sleepy People HMV BD-5437*,
 EA-2244*
OEA-6966-1 Is That The Way To Treat A HMV BD-5438*
 Sweetheart?
OEA-6967-1 Colorado Sunset   –   *, EA-2230*
OEA-6968-2 While A Cigarette Was Burning HMV BD-5437*,
 EA-2251*
                                       London, December 16, 1938.
OEA-7264-1 Any Broken Hearts To Mend? HMV BD-5443*
OEA-7265-1 Summer's End   –   *, EA-2251*
OEA-7266-1 My Own HMV BD-5444*
OEA-7267-1 You're As Pretty As A Picture   –   *
                                       London, January 10, 1939.
OEA-7272-1 They Say HMV BD-5448*,
 EA-2265*
OEA-7273-1 If Ever A Heart Was In The Right Place –   *, EA-2292*
OEA-7274-1 One Day When We Were Young HMV BD-5449*
OEA-7275-2 I'm In Love With Vienna   –   *
                                       London, February 3, 1939.
OEA-7293-1 Grandma Said HMV BD-5457*,
 EA-2327*
OEA-7294-1 Deep In A Dream   –   *, EA-2292*
OEA-7295-1 You're A Sweet Little Headache HMV BD-5458*,
 EA-2289*
With REGINALD WILLIAMS AND HIS FUTURISTS.
                                       London, February 8, 1939.
CA-17345-1 I'm Madly In Love With You   Col FB-2167
 NOTE: Al Bowlly does not sing on other titles from this session.
Acc. by orchestra. London, February 14, 1939.
OEA-7298-1 Romany HMV BD-666, EA-2370
OEA-7299-1 Lonely   –   –
OEA-7562-1 I Miss You In The Morning HMV BD-673
OEA-7563-1 Violin In Vienna   –
 NOTE: Matrices OEA-7300/7561 inclusive are by other artists on other dates.

With GERALDO AND HIS ORCHESTRA. London, March 7, 1939.
OEA-7611-1 The Same Old Story HMV BD-5467*
OEA-7612-1 Could Be HMV BD-5468*,
 EA-2237*
OEA-7613-1 Between A Kiss and A Sigh   –   *
                                       London, April 4, 1939.
OEA-7628-1 To Mother, With Love HMV BD-5473,
 EA-2349

OEA-7629-2	Waltz Of My Heart	Rejected
OEA-7630-1	Thanks For Everything	HMV BD-5472
OEA-7631-1	I Miss You In The Morning	HMV BD-5473

NOTE: Matrix OEA-7629-1, issued on HMV BD-5472, has no vocal refrain.

With REGINALD WILLIAMS AND HIS FUTURISTS.

London, May 5, 1939.

CA-17438-1	Small Town	Col FB-2226
CA-17439-1	What Do You Know About Love?	Col FB-2227

NOTE: Al Bowlly does not sing on other titles from this session.

Acc. by orchestra.   London, May 11, 1939.

OEA-7854-2	What Do You Know About Love?	HMV BD-706, EA-2404
OEA-7855-1	Hey Gypsy, Play Gypsy	HMV BD-709
OEA-7856-1	South Of The Border	HMV BD-706, EA-2395
OEA-7857-1	Dark Eyes	HMV BD-709, EA-2524

With BRAM MARTIN AND HIS BAND.   London, June 8, 1939.

R-3678-1	The Waves Of The Ocean Are Whispering Goodnight	Rex 9590*, Kristall 22056*

NOTE: Al Bowlly does not sing on other titles from this session.

Acc. by orchestra directed by Ronnie Munro.

London, October 5, 1939.

OEA-8111-1	Moon Love	HMV BD-762, EA-2452
OEA-8112-1	Au Revoir But Not Goodbye	– –
OEA-8113-1	A Man And His Dream	HMV BD-776
OEA-8114-1	Ridin' Home	– EA-2545

London, December 21, 1939.

OEA-8334-1	Bella Bambina	HMV BD-808
OEA-8335-1	Over The Rainbow	–
OEA-8336-1	Somewhere In France With You	HMV BD-805, EA-2515
OEA-8337-1	Give Me My Ranch	– –

NOTE: The last title is given on HMV EA-2515 as 'Alla En El Rancho Grande (My Ranch)'.

London, February 15, 1940.

OEA-8475-1	It's A Lovely Day Tomorrow	HMV BD-828
OEA-8476-1	Careless	–

With MAURICE WINNICK AND HIS ORCHESTRA.

London, March 1, 1940.

OEA-8382-1	Chatterbox	HMV BD-5572
OEA-8383-1	When You Wish Upon A Star	HMV BD-5573
OEA-8385-1	Turn On The Old Music Box	–

Acc. by orchestra.   London, March 7, 1940.

OEA-8500-1	Dreaming	HMV BD-834, EA-2684
OEA-8505-1	A Little Rain Must Fall	HMV BD-827
OEA-8506-1	When You Wear Your Sunday Blue	– EA-2545

OEA-8551-1   Walkin' Thru' Mockin' Bird Lane   HMV BD-834
    NOTE: Matrices OEA-8501/4 and OEA-8507/50 inclusive are by other artists on other dates.

With MAURICE WINNICK AND HIS ORCHESTRA.
                                    London, March 26, 1940.
OEA-8570-1   Who's Taking You Home Tonight?   HMV BD-5582*,
                                              EA-2539*
OEA-8571-1   Arm In Arm   HMV BD-5583*,
                                              120944* (Can.)
OEA-8572-1   There's A Boy Coming Home On   -* EA-2569* - *
             Leave
OEA-8573-1   My Capri Serenade   HMV BD-5582* -*

With KEN 'SNAKEHIPS' JOHNSON AND HIS WEST INDIAN ORCHESTRA and THE HENDERSON TWINS.   London, April 24, 1940.
OEA-8582-1   Blow, Blow, Thou Winter Wind   HMV BD-5592*,
                                              EA-2871*
OEA-8583-1   It Was A Lover And His Lass   _   *   _   *

Duets with JIMMY MESENE, acc. by their own guitars.
                                    London, July 18, 1940.
OEA-8840-1   Make Love With A Guitar; When   HMV BD-857
             I Dream Of Home
OEA-8841-2   Make-Believe Island; The Woodpecker -
             Song

                                    London, September 12, 1940.
OEA-8741-2   Turn Your Money In Your Pocket; HMV BD-865
             I'll Never Smile Again; We'll Go Smiling Along
OEA-8742-2   I'm Stepping Out With A Memory   -
             Tonight; I Haven't Time To Be A Millionaire

                                    London, December 6, 1940.
OEA-9058-1   Ferry Boat Serenade   HMV BD-892
OEA-9059-1   Only Forever   -

                                    London, April 2, 1941.
OEA-9226-1   Nicky The Greek (Has Gone)   HMV BD-922
OEA-9227-1   When That Man Is Dead And Gone   -

Two weeks later, Al Bowlly was killed in an air-raid on London.

INDEX

Abriani, John, 13
Adeler, Edgar, 4–6, 11–13, 28
Allen, Les, 27, 29
Ambrose, 18, 24, 27, 34, 36, 37, 39, 58, 60, 104
American Federation of Musicians, 81, 82
Amos 'n' Andy, 85
Ampier, Nick, 7
Andrews Sisters, 103
Armstrong, Louis, 82
Aronsohn, Abe, 82
Auckland, Lord, 109

Bacon, Max, 58
Bag o' Nails, The, 18, 50
Bailey, Derek, 94
Barrigo, Don, 12, 94, 100, 104
Barry, Jean, 21
Batten, Reg, 15, 19
Beiderbecke, Bix, 15
Benito, Mario, 12
Benny, Jack, 91
Berigan, Bunny, 31
Berlin, Irving, 106
Berly, Harry, 61, 73
Bowlly, Al, birth of, 1; schooldays, 2; as barber, 3; with Adeler band, 4–6; with Lequime band, 6–10; in Germany, 11–14; in London, with Elizalde band, 18–26; busking, 30; with Roy Fox band, 32–33; with Ray Noble band, 37–38; at The Monseigneur, 41–48; first marriage, 49–54; with Lew Stone band, 59–70; in films, 71; in Scheveningen, 73, 74; solo act, 75; on tour, 77–78; to USA, 80; at the Rainbow Room, 84–88; second marriage, 89; with 'Radio City Rhythm Makers', 94–96; freelance, 98–104; death, 108
Bowlly, Misch, 2, 94, 97
Bradley, Will, 85
Brannigan, Owen, 71
Briggs, Arthur, 13
Bristol Coliseum, 78
Brown, Sidney, 101
Browne, Sam, 27, 37, 97, 103
Buchanan, Jack, 40
Buckman, Sid, 32, 59, 104
Bullock, Capt. Talbot, 107
Burns and Allan, 85, 91

Butlin, Billy, 98
BBC, 15, 18, 20

Café Anglais, the, 39, 53, 76
Café de Paris, the, 31, 76, 106
Café Royal, the, 18
Calcutta, 6–10
Carhart, George, 13
Carlisle, Elsie, 37
Carlton Hotel, the, 18
Carmichael, Hoagy, 42
Carroll, Eddie, 61
Casa Loma Orchestra, the, 92
Cecil Hotel, the, 18
Chez Henri, 18
Ciro's, 18
Cock, Gerald, 42
Colin, Sid, 100
Collins, Al, 19, 25
Collins, Lottie, 3
Como, Perry, 93
Confrey, Zez, 35
Cooper, Lady Diana, 42
Cortesi Brothers, the, 54
Costa, Sam, 103
Cotton, Billy, 27
Courtneidge, Cecily, 97
Coward, Noël, 42, 47, 59
Craven, Earl of, 52
Crazy Gang, the, 67
Crosby, Bing, 65, 85, 92
Crossman, Joe, 1, 60–64, 67, 76, 102, 104, 105

Dalton, Murray, 50
Daly, Betty, 64
d'Amato, Chappie, 99, 100, 108
d'Andrea, Danny, 85, 91
Davis, Ben, 18
Davis, Bobby, 16, 19, 24
Davis, Joe, 98
Davis, Lew, 36, 60, 61, 64, 66, 68, 73, 74
De Clifford, Lord, 52
De Falla, Manuel, 26
Dennis, Denny, 103
Dix, Otto, 11
Dorchester, the, 39
Dorsey Brothers, the, 61, 79, 84, 90. 92, 93
Dubois, Mme, 7

161

Easton, Jim, 61, 67
Eberle, Bob, 92, 93
Eberle, Ray, 93
Elizalde, Fred, 13, 15–26
Ellington, Duke, 61
Eloff Street, 3
Elwin, Maurice, 82
Empire, Shepherds Bush, 1
Holborn, 67

Fagan, Gideon, 30
Fairbanks, Douglas, 64
Farley, Max, 21, 24
Ferrie, Joe, 32, 57, 61
Ferrie, Miff, 95
Fields, Gracie, 67, 98
Fillis, Len, 4, 5, 13, 24, 38
Firman, Bert, 35
Firpo's Restaurant, 13
Fitzgerald, Ella, 93
Fitzgibbons, Dave, 21
Fleming, Jock, 38
Formby, George, 67
Fox, Roy, 1, 31–33, 37, 38, 39–46, 56–60, 61, 76, 82, 104
Frankel, Ben, 19
Frascati's, 18
Freeman, Bud, 84, 86

Gaden, Robert, 11
Gardner, Freddie, 73
Gargoyle Club, the, 18
Gay, Noel, 101
Geraldo, 24, 97, 100, 101, 103, 104
Gibbons, Carroll, 34, 36, 39, 82
Goddard, Sgt., 51
Goldberg, Max, 36
Gonella, Nat, 1, 32, 35, 37, 41, 42, 45, 49, 50, 53, 57, 58, 61, 67, 68, 72, 73, 74, 75, 92, 94, 95, 103, 104
Gold, Harry, 104
Goodman, Al, 88
Goodman, Benny, 92
Gordon, Harry, 28
Gorney, Jay, 33
Gray, Glen, 92
Green, Bert, 95
Gregg, Desmond, 5
Grosz, George, 11

Halek, Vic, 7
Hall, Henry, 37
Hambone, the, 18
Hampton, Percy, 94
Harburg, Y. P., 33
Harding, Hilda, 68, 69
Harding, Lesley, 68, 69
Harrie, Albert, 37
Harris, Jack, 76, 82, 104
Harris, Phil, 91
Harty, Bill, 32, 36, 37, 38, 61, 63, 67, 73, 80, 81, 83, 84, 88

Hawkins, Coleman, 82
Hayes, Harry, 16, 21
Haymes, Dick, 93
Helen, 99, 105, 108–10
Henderson, Chick, 103, 109
Henderson Twins, the, 103
Heyman, Eddie, 87
Hines, Harry, 38
Holliday, Billie, 93
Hopkins, Dan, 6
Houghton, Bill, 7
Howard, Sydney, 71
Hudson, Harry, 29, 35
Hughes, Spike, 38
Hulbert, Claude, 71
Hulbert, Jack, 97
Hurley, George, 17, 19
Hutchinson, Leslie, 106
Hylton, Jack, 19, 21, 22, 27, 34, 36, 37, 44, 60, 79, 82, 103

Irwin, Pee Wee, 84, 90, 91

Jacobs, Johnny, 4, 5
Jacobson, Harry, 37
Jacobson, Jock, 104
Jackson, Jack, 34, 39
Jackson, Leslie, 51, 52
Jackson, Stanley, 17
James, Harry, 93
Johannesburg, 1, 3, 4
Johnson, Ken 'Snakehips', 103, 104, 106
Joynson-Hicks, Sir William, 51

Kane, Alan, 97
Kapinsky, Ernie, 97
Kaplan, Delmar, 84
Kemp, Hal, 31
Kinnoull, Lord, 52
Kit-Kat Club, the, 18, 31, 69
Knight, Nobby, 19
Krupa, Gene, 93
Kyser, Kay, 93
Kunz, Charlie, 18, 82

Lane, Lupino, 101
Lang, Eddie, 15
Lawrence, Mr Justice, 60
Lee, Len, 19
Lee, Peggy, 93
Lequime, Jimmy, 7–10
Lewis, Edward, 31
Lillie, Beatrice, 105, 109
Lindrum, Horace, 98
Lipton, Sidney, 34, 97
Liter, Monia, 1, 7–10, 64, 65, 75, 100, 102, 105, 108
Livingston, Fud, 21, 25
Lombardo, Guy, 65
Lorenzi, Mario, 19
Loss, Joe, 103
Lynn, Vera, 103

MacDonald, Jeanette, 64
Mackey, Percival, 23, 27
Maguire, Claude 'Sax', 7–10
Mairants, Ivor, 104
Mandell, Pete, 37
Mantovani, 42, 97, 98
Margetson, Stella, 50, 51
Marjie, 64, 65, 69, 73, 74, 82, 83, 84, 88–91, 99
Martin, Bram, 102
Maugham, Somerset, 9
Mayfair Hotel, the, 18, 39
Maxwell, Dick, 16, 18
MCA, 79
McCardle, Mr Justice, 61
McCarthy, Albert, 25
McLaglen, Victor, 64
Mehring, Walter, 11
Melachrino, George, 104
Melody Maker, 4, 18, 20, 21, 24, 43, 56, 57, 61, 70, 75, 80, 81, 93, 97, 109
Mendelssohn, Felix, 97
Merman, Ethel, 85
Mesene, Jimmy, 103, 106–9
Meyrick, Kate, 50–2
Miller, Glenn, 84–87, 90–91, 93
Mills, Annette, 101
Mills Brothers, the, 103
Mince, Johnny, 84, 86, 90, 91
Miranda, Jack, 19
Mole, Miff, 15
Monseigneur Restaurant, The, 39–47, 53, 56–66, 68, 76
Munich, 11–14
Munro, Ronnie, 97

Neagle, Anna, 71
Negri, Pola, 25
Nichols, Red, 15
Noakes, Alfie, 60, 61, 73, 104
Noble, Ray, 2, 30, 35–38, 65, 66, 68, 71, 72, 73–75, 78–92, 102

Oakie, Jack, 85
O'Connor, Cavan, 27
Oliver, Vic, 98
O'Malley, Pat, 27, 37
Oppenheimer, Mrs Louis, 17
Original Dixieland Jazz Band, the, 82
Owen, Rex, 16

Pavilion, Shepherds Bush, 24
Payne, Jack, 18, 24, 27, 34
Payne, Norman, 16, 21, 36, 37
Petrillo, James Caesar, 93
Phillips, Sid, 104
Phillips, Van, 22
Piccadilly Hotel, the, 18
Pink, Reg, 37
Pisani, Nick, 85
Plant, Jack, 97
Pogson, 'Poggy', 104

Polo, Danny, 82
Pougnet, Jean, 36
Prince of Wales, the, 31, 42
Prospero, Fritz, 85
Pursglove, Reg, 36

Quealey, Chelsea, 16

Rabin, Oscar, 97, 104
Raffles Hotel, 8–10
Raffles, Sir Stamford, 9
Rainbow Room, the, 79–89
Ralton, Bert, 10, 15
Ravel, 26
Rawalpindi, 6
Redlich, Joseph, 12
Rey, Monte, 103
Ritte, Ernest, 32, 37, 61, 64, 68
Robey, George, 21
Roberts, Freda, 49–55
Rockwell O'Keefe Bureau, 78–79 81, 83
Rollini, Adrian, 16, 19, 24
Rollini, Arthur, 16, 19, 24
Romano's, 18
Rosebury, Arthur, 18
Rosing, Val, 27
Ross, Fred, 13
Roy, Harry, 39, 76
Rusin, Jack, 19

Sabini Brothers, the, 54
San Marco, the, 39
Sarawak, the Maharanee of, 42, 53
Sargent, Kenny, 92
Savoy Hotel, the, 15–20, 39
Scheveningen, 73–75
Schwitzenberg, Glenn and Wilbur, 84
Scott-Coomber, Billy, 27
Shakespeare, Bill, 104
Shalson, Harry, 27
Shaw, Artie, 92, 93
Shaw, G. B. S., 102
Sheldon, Eddie, 17, 18
Siday, Eric, 36
Silver Slipper, the, 18
Simon, George T., 79, 84–87, 92
Sims, Ginny, 93
Sinatra, Frank, 93
Slavin, Archie, 94
Smith, George, 19, 36
Somers, Debroy, 15
Sourabaya, 5
Speelman, Joe, 7–10
Spivak, Charlie, 84, 85
Stafford, Jo, 93
Stamp, Lord and Lady, 109
Starita, Al, 18, 27, 28
Starita, Ray, 37
Sterling, Louis, 80
Stock, 'Tiny', 17
Stone, Joyce, 39–41, 45–47, 62, 66, 97, 109

163